Robert S. Wood

Mountain Cabin

Illustrated by Lewis E. Jones

Chronicle Books   San Francisco

Illustrations by Lewis E. Jones
Printed in the United States of America

Library of Congress Cataloging in Publication Data
Wood, Robert Snyder, 1930-
   Mountain cabin.
    1. Natural history—Outdoor books.   I.   Title.
QH81.W727   500.9′2′4   76-30878
ISBN 0-87701-090-0

Chronicle Books
870 Market Street
San Francisco
California 94102

Contents

Preface

Where is *Granite Basin*? Granite Basin is real; so are the people and incidents described. But in order to protect the basin's fragile character—as well as the privacy of my neighbors and myself—I have concealed its identity and disguised its location.

Since we purchased the cabin there have been many changes, and not all have been for the better. Government inspectors have discovered the basin, and they increasingly disapprove our rustic, functional but often nonconforming cabins. Outhouses have been banned; we are urged to build a sewer; there is threatening talk of bringing in a road. We have even been offered 'electrification.'

More people have come, the season has lengthened and bigger motorboats churn the lakes each summer. The gentle sounds of wind in the trees and water lapping on the rocks are harder now to hear. Clearly, Granite cannot stand much more use.

But do not imagine the basin has lost its charm or been spoiled. It hasn't. It remains wild and lovely, free of electricity, pollution and cars. On the edge of a high western wilderness it is still a Shangri-La.

ONE

Discovery

The words "mountain cabin" have held strong appeal ever since I was a boy, when I read exciting tales of the mountain men and looked at pictures of their wilderness cabins. Those stories made me dream of a snug little hut far back in the woods by a mountain lake, where I could live forever.

As I grew the dream took more definite shape: I needed pine trees and trout, snow in the winter, and room to paddle a canoe. My cabin must lie beyond the farthest road, accessible only by boat or trail, with no electricity, telephone, or doorbell to disturb the peace of the wilds. Over the years I filled notebooks with drawings and floor plans.

Once I was old enough and had saved a few dollars I spent several summers looking at mountain cabins, but I never found anything I wanted to own. The older I grew, the more cabins I looked at, the less likely it seemed I would find what I wanted, and after a few years I stopped looking. The dream was lying dormant in the back of my mind when I married. When my wife expressed a willingness to try an overnight trip beyond the roads in the mountains, I searched for the ideal place to take her.

It wasn't just the wilderness that interested Freda. She wanted to find out what it was about the mountains that drew me so strongly. Because I hoped she would share my affection for the wilds, I had to find a place that was beautiful but reasonably gentle. It wouldn't matter much if we didn't have it to ourselves —in fact she might be glad to see a few people. I studied my maps and talked to several friends and finally settled on the wilderness country behind Granite Basin, though I'd been there only once.

It wasn't the high, wild timberline where I spent most of my free time in the summer, but it was lovely and wild in a friendly way, and its glaciated granite gave it the look of much higher country. It ought to give Freda an enjoyable first backpacking trip.

It was late July when we reached Granite Basin, a steep-walled granite bowl hollowed out by glaciers, with two connecting lakes in the bottom. Though the morning sun was hot, snow still lay in patches on the mountains above us. At the end of the road stood a rustic lodge on the shore of Lower Granite, and we parked.

In Granite Chalet we ate a leisurely breakfast by an open window, watching the boats come and go in the harbor, then we picked up our packs and walked down to the dock. Three or four people were sitting in an old wooden launch with the outboard motor running. Since the boat trip up the basin would save three miles of walking and add another dimension to the trip, we decided to ride.

As the boat moved up the lake the basin opened out. To the left the steep slope was thick with dark hemlock. On our right granite cliffs rose a thousand feet to a crest that seemed to overhang the lake. The boatman called it Eagle Peak. Beyond it and higher at the head of the lake, rose squat and massive Granite Peak.

Halfway up the lake cabins began to appear among the trees along the shore. They were small and unpainted, with shake walls and roofs that had weathered like the granite around them. Rowboats and canoes were moored below at small docks. Smoke rose from several stone chimneys.

We had nearly reached shore at the head of the lake and seemed about to run aground when an opening appeared in a clump of lodgepole pine. We slowed to a crawl and slipped into a tree-shaded channel barely large enough for the boat. Willow and mountain ash grew out over the water. The boat chugged slowly upstream, winding through clear pools joined by narrow runs, and after no more than a hundred yards we emerged between two boulders into Upper Granite Lake.

Where the lower lake had been long and narrow with a smoothly curving shore, Upper Granite was small and rounded and cut into a series of bays and coves. Adding to the contrast were half a dozen islands. Tucked among the trees and perched on the points a number of cabins were spaced at comfortable intervals along the wooded shore. At the head of the lake we landed and started up the trail that led out of the basin and into the wilderness beyond.

But my mind stayed behind on the shores of Granite Lakes. The cabins in the basin, it dawned on me now, were accessible only by trail or boat. And there was no electricity beyond the Chalet at the end of the road. The lakes, which held trout, froze over in the winter when heavy snowfall buried the basin. The more I thought about those cabins the more excited I became.

Granite Basin fitted my dream. This might be the place.

I had never told Freda about my long-held hope of one day owning a cabin in the mountains. There hadn't been any occasion. Chances of fulfillment seemed too remote, and speaking of my hopes only brought me frustration. But that night in our camp, with all the eloquence I could summon, I told her of my dream of having a haven from the pressures of the city, a place to spend weekends and vacations in all seasons, a permanent base to anchor my life, a home in the land that I thought of as home. And so forth.

Freda listened patiently. After all, she had hoped to find out why mountain country moved me. Now she heard me asking her to share my dream, to understand my need for a mountain cabin, to give her blessing to my quest for a place at Granite Lakes. To make the idea appealing I mentioned fresh trout for breakfast (which she loved), an unparalleled environment for our children-to-be, escape from our small city apartment, refuge from the sight and sound of automobiles, a place to swing in a hammock and feed the squirrels, where doorbells and telephones would never ring.

When I had finished my speech I anxiously asked what she thought. Much of what I'd said was strange and perplexing to her, but she found the country pretty, she liked Granite Basin, and she thought it might be fun to have a cabin of our own— even though she was wary of the primitive housekeeping I so romantically called "simple." She knew who would have to keep house and do the cooking. But she was willing to give it a try.

On our return to the Chalet I began the search at once. It didn't take long to find the two men who occasionally handled the sale of Granite cabins, but what they had to tell me was discouraging. Lots of people wanted them and none were for sale. Most cabins were still owned by the families that had built them forty or fifty years before. Those few that were sold usually went to family or very close friends and never appeared on the market. Our best chance, I was told, was to try to find a cabin to rent. We might in time become acquainted with a cabinowner who would consider selling.

The outlook was bleak, but from the city I continued to call and write my contacts to make sure they didn't forget me. That September we were invited to come look at an expensive lakeside lot that was snarled in litigation and of questionable zoning, but might someday be for sale. We were glad for an excuse to return to Granite Basin, but the lot turned out to be hopeless.

Then one Friday afternoon late in October we received a call from a lady we had met on the September trip. Bea had heard just that morning of a cabin for sale at the foot of Upper Granite. A childless older couple had unexpectedly decided to sell. The cabin itself was described as rundown, but the site was supposed to be unusually nice. She was passing it up because she still hoped to build.

I called the agent right away, learned the price and terms, and made an appointment to see the cabin at nine the following morning. We set the alarm and left the city before dawn, reaching the basin a few minutes early. It was a fine fall day but a sharpness in the air warned that winter was approaching. The surface of the lake had dropped five feet, exposing a band of grey rock along the shore. The Chalet was closed and shuttered, the harbor was almost empty and the place looked deserted. Much of the friendliness of summer was gone.

We started up the lake with the agent in his boat. A sprinkling of aspen stood out like yellow flames in the dark hemlock forest on our left. The lake was down, said the agent, because the power company owned the top five feet of water and took it every fall after everyone was gone. At the head of the lake we beached the boat near the mouth of the now dry channel and started through the trees toward Upper Granite. As we walked the agent told us about the property. Casually he concluded, "The cabin, of course, will have to come down."

"Have to come down!" I said. "Why?"

The place, he explained, had been neglected for years and a really severe winter would probably crush it flat. "The snow here, you know, gets twenty feet deep. The cabin could go any time. Better to tear it down and start fresh." As though to illustrate his point he stopped and pointed. We looked down through the trees into a hollow between two granite bluffs. Nestled in the rock sat a weather-beaten building with shake-

11

covered walls and a crumbling shingle roof. Peeling brown shutters covered windows and doors, and a tilting rusty stovepipe stuck through the roof.

Moving closer we could see that two rectangular buildings, each with a peaked roof, had been pushed or built together at right angles to form a stubby T-shaped cabin. The hollow in which it sat opened out into a small grassy flat, shaded by pines, that extended to the shore of a lovely little cove on Upper Granite. A path from the cabin led through knee-deep grass to a pair of big logs that served as a primitive dock.

The lot, said the agent, fronted on both the channel and the lake, so either could be used as a harbor. He pointed out a two-hole outhouse concealed in a draw fifty feet above the cabin, and he observed that the cabin site offered exceptional privacy. Neighboring cabins were well removed, and nearly out of sight, thanks to conveniently located screens of pine forest. When we had circled the cabin the agent sat down on a rock and invited us to look around further.

"We'd like to see inside," I said. "You've got the keys?"

"It's closed up tight for the winter," he said without moving. "Besides, it's a mess inside, and dark. Take my word for it, it isn't worth saving."

"From the outside," I said, "it doesn't look that bad. If you've got the keys, I'd like to take a look."

Reluctantly he got up, produced a ring of keys, opened the padlock that held the shutter in place, and unlocked the battered green door that stood behind it. Then he stepped aside and waved us in. I walked into the darkness and immediately crashed into a rocking chair heaped with dusty lawn furniture.

From outside on the porch the agent volunteered that the shutters unhooked from inside. Freda found her way to a window, raised the sash, and opened a shutter to dimly light the room. Now that we could see, it wasn't hard to understand why the agent hadn't wanted us inside. The room was so crammed with dusty furniture and junk it was nearly impossible to move. There were wicker chairs, rickety tables, an iron stove, stools and benches, dismantled iron beds, a treadle sewing machine, and several bedsprings—all thickly covered with dust.

Buckled wall paneling was plastered with curling magazine

pictures and old religious calendars. A plate rail heaped with trash circled the room at eye level. The battered fly-specked windows were festooned with cobwebs, and broken panes had been ingeniously patched by gluing more glass over cracks and holes. When I asked about a loft the agent, who had been glumly watching from the doorway, picked up a stick and deftly released the free end of a hinged ladder that had been hooked against the water-stained ceiling.

I climbed through a black hole in the ceiling into a network of cobwebs and lighted a match. A narrow half-floored attic, criss-crossed with bracing, lay half an inch deep in dust. Light from hundreds of holes in the roof illumined a scattering of junk. Somewhere nearby a mouse gnawed loudly. No one could possibly have spent the night in that space. "It's got possibilities," I called truthfully to Freda, and descended.

Leaving the bedroom-parlor, we forced our way into the darkened kitchen. Freda, who was leading, bumped into something soft and swinging, and jumped back with a gasp. I lit another match. Dangling from the rafters by a rope was a rolled-up mattress shrouded in canvas. "That's to protect it from the mice," explained the agent.

We opened another shutter and looked around. Though the parlor had contained enough furniture for two cabins, the kitchen was equally crammed. The only way the owners could have made space enough to live was to move all the furniture outside when they visited. Freda was inspecting the cooking facilities with mingled distaste and disbelief. In one sooty corner, covered in cobwebs, stood a huge, greasy, black-iron woodburning stove. A deep washtub sink beside it drained directly into a blackened bucket underneath.

"But where are the faucets?" she asked the agent.

"The owners," he said archly, "were content to dip their water from the lake."

A sagging tin icebox, still ripe with the odors of long-departed food, stood in a shed-like pantry so ramshackle that mice, squirrels, and even birds came and went as they pleased. Pots and pans were scattered on the floor beside a half-filled woodbox that had become a large mouse nest. The paneling on the walls was coming loose here and there and the ceiling was sagging, but tin can lids had been nailed over knotholes in a vain attempt to keep out the wildlife. There was only one small counter and the owners had done without gas as well as water and plumbing.

Freda began to cough from the dust and the agent tactfully suggested we return to the fresh air and sunlight. By this time we were happy to follow. When the shutter door was once again locked in place the agent remembered an errand. Before he disappeared he invited us to take another look at the marvelous site. We stood there looking at the cabin. I tried desperately to think of something positive to say.

"I suppose it's *just* what you've been looking for," said Freda.

"I know it's a mess," I helplessly began. My face, I suppose, did not conceal my anguish. Freda was smiling.

"If it's really what you want," she said, "it's all right with me."

At that moment the agent reappeared from the draw.

"We'll buy it," I said, "at your price."

"That's fine," he said, frowning at his watch. "But now we've got to get back. I've got an appointment to show it to another party at eleven."

I looked at him and saw he was serious. "But you can't," I said, "it's sold."

He put his head down and started for the boat. "I'm sorry," he said. "I promised they could see it at eleven."

I couldn't believe it. The cabin, within my grasp, was slipping away. I caught up with him and stopped, blocking his path. "Look," I said firmly. "You offered the cabin at a certain price and terms. We've accepted that offer and that constitutes a deal. The cabin is sold. We'll go with you to meet the other party and explain. Then we'll go to your place and I'll give you a check and get your receipt. Then we'll call the owners and tell them the cabin's been sold."

He stood there a moment looking past me at the lake. "All right," he said slowly. "I guess that's all right."

And that's the way it happened. When the paperwork was done he called the owner long distance and introduced me with surprising enthusiasm. When I got on the line I told the old gentleman how happy we were, and I asked about taking possession. He said he and his wife would like to make one last visit to collect a few personal belongings, but with winter so close it was

14

too late this year. If we could wait until the ice went out next spring, we could make the official transfer then. That way we'd have the cabin all next summer, and the down-payment wouldn't be due for six months.

In the effort to get the cabin I hadn't given any thought to where the money would come from. I knew I'd get it somewhere if I found what I wanted. Now suddenly that problem was solved. In six months' time, with both of us working, we could save what we needed to augment our savings. When I told the old gentleman how perfect that sounded he said he'd decided, since we were paying full price, to throw in his twelve-foot boat and five-horse outboard, which were in storage.

When I thanked him and said goodbye the agent served us coffee and offered his hearty congratulations. "You're the first people who've seen that little cabin's real potential," he said, beaming. "Basically, it's perfectly sound. A little fixing up and you'll have yourselves a really fine place." He shook my hand warmly as we left.

I still have to smile when I recall that crazy day and how awful the cabin looked—and how badly I wanted it.

TWO

The First Summer

The winter that followed was one of growing antic-
ipation and excitement. In the spring the five-horse outboard
arrived, but it wasn't big enough for our purpose. With all the
hauling we'd have to do, we were going to need more power. So
I traded in the little engine on an ancient, enormous sixteen-
horsepower Johnson. The rewind starter was gone, the gas tank
was caved in, and the throttle was unpredictable, but it was
suitably powerful and our total cash outlay was only thirty dollars.

On May twenty-fifth the agent called to say the ice had gone
out the previous week and the sellers had made their visit to
collect their personal belongings. Since we had made the down-
payment and signed all the papers the place was now ours. We
could stop by and pick up the keys anytime. We said we'd be up
Saturday for the three-day Memorial Day weekend.

We arrived in the morning with a carload of camping equipment, the big white outboard filling the back seat, and food
enough for a week. The agent told us that Jorgy, the Chalet's
proprietor, would be looking for us down at the dock. I'd met
him years before on a snow camping trip to the basin.

It had seemed like midsummer on the drive to the mountains,
but when we entered Granite Basin we encountered deep snow.
The road to the Chalet had been cleared just a week and the
snowbanks stood higher than the car. Eagle Peak and the sunny
north shore were entirely free of snow, but the basin's south side
was a wintry unbroken white.

The Chalet was closed and the place looked deserted, but as
soon as we parked Jorgy appeared, a lean, weathered man in a

faded plaid shirt. He helped us load our heap of supplies into one of the boat taxis, and on top of the white outboard he printed WOOD in grease pencil. He promised to launch our boat, mount the motor and check it out, then bring it up the lake on Monday morning so we could use it coming out that afternoon. Then he drove us up the lake in the taxi and unloaded us at the dock beside the channel. We watched his hunched figure guide the boat back down the lake, then we each picked up a bundle and headed through the snow toward the cabin. Freda, though three months pregnant, insisted on carrying a full load.

It was exciting to see the cabin again, now that it was ours— the first home we had owned. On that bright spring morning it looked wonderful. A snowdrift still covered more than half the back porch, but the shutters were swung back and there were curtains in the windows. A lively stream poured from the draw that hid the outhouse, cascaded downhill to flow beneath the cabin and flood the grassy flat on the way to Upper Granite. I put down my load, turned the key in the lock, and waved Freda inside with a flourish.

Sunlight streamed in the windows to reveal the incredible accumulation we remembered. If the sellers had taken away keepsakes they were small ones. After clearing off a table, I set up and lighted the gasoline stove we had brought, drew a bucket of water from the lake, and put it on to heat for coffee. Then I portaged our remaining supplies from Lower Granite.

Freda made coffee and unpacked the lunch while I buried a bucket in the back porch snowbank to serve as a refrigerator for our milk, meat, eggs and cheese. Then we took our lunch out onto the sunny granite bluff that formed a low wall between the cabin and the lake. The entire upper basin was one unbroken snowfield from the tops of the peaks to the water, but the air was still and warm and the bright sky was cloudless.

Our stomachs well filled, we were eager to go to work, Freda in the kitchen while I attacked the parlor-bedroom. We opened both doors and all the windows, and soon the cabin's musty odor gave way to pine-fresh mountain air. I set to work carrying excess furniture outdoors until there was room to move around, then I swept the contents of the plate rail into empty cardboard boxes which I set aside for future sorting.

17

Meanwhile, Freda in the kitchen was sorting through a pile of plates, cups, pots and pans—far more than we needed. She was pleased with the old-fashioned kitchenware she found, exclaiming with delight over pieces more common in museums than stores, and busily making lists of what the kitchen still needed. I was equally lucky at finding valuable tools, and we called to one another at each fresh discovery, chattering like children about the treasures we found.

About midafternoon the bright sunshine vanished. Huge cumulus clouds boiled above the basin, blocking out the sun, and it quickly turned chill. In the kitchen I winnowed the mouse nests from the woodpile and kindled a fire in the big Wedgewood cookstove which very soon warmed up the room. Returning to the parlor, I assembled the best-looking double bedsprings and mattress I could find, then I carried half a dozen moth-eaten army blankets outdoors, shook them and spread them to air on the granite. We had brought along sleeping bags, but the blankets, together with cotton flannel sheets, would keep us comfortably warm and we decided to sleep on what the cabin provided. It seemed a little like living off the land.

When the bed was made I hauled in wood for the stove and brought in the meat from the snowbank for dinner. The air outside had grown cold and the last of the blue sky was filling with cloud. The steel-colored lake and snowy shores now held a strong suggestion of winter, and I was glad to return to the cheerful kitchen with its roaring stove. While Freda made dinner I filled and lighted our two gas lanterns, hanging them from nails I found in the rafters, set the table with candles and poured out two glasses of sherry.

After dinner we washed the dishes and pulled our chairs close to the glowing stove to read, but before long we were happily talking and adding to our lists of "things to get." A shopping trip to the nearest store meant a trip by boat or trail to the car at the Chalet, followed by a fifteen mile drive over a mountain pass. So our lists needed to be reasonably complete. Unable to sit still while there were new possessions to examine, I opened the big Victrola and found dozens of old seventy-eight records, most of them forty or fifty years old. Dusting off the cactus needle and winding the crank, I put on a record. From out of the past came

Alexander's Ragtime Band in a bouncy arrangement that made us both laugh. The beat was so compelling it set us Charlestoning in our warm smoky kitchen. After dancing our way through *The Varsity Drag* and *You Were Meant For Me* we had grown so warm and winded—we had forgotten the air was so thin at this altitude—that we were glad to go outside to cool off.

It was utterly still and the sky was thick with low-lying cloud. We went out onto the bluff to look around the basin. Since the shoreline was dark we apparently had the upper lake to ourselves. Although at first the night seemed still, we gradually grew aware of the sounds of running water. The stream beneath the cabin murmured softly in the dark and the roar of a waterfall echoed around the basin. From somewhere nearby the croaking of thousands of frogs pulsated in the darkness. When the cold began to penetrate we went back inside for a pot of tea before bed. After the warmth of the kitchen, the bedroom was like a butcher's walk-in icebox.

When we woke the next morning it was colder still. Our breath made clouds of steam in the still, dry air. When thirst finally drove me from the blankets, I discovered with delight that two inches of snow had fallen in the night. I hurried shivering to the gasoline stove and put on coffee water, then I built a wood fire in the Wedgewood, nursing it while I waited for the water to boil. When the coffee was made I packed the big stove with all the wood it would hold and hurried back to bed with the two steaming mugs. Deep beneath the covers we waited in comfort for the kitchen to warm before rushing in to dress by the stove.

All that day we spent working on the cabin: sweeping, burning, dusting, sorting. It kept us busy but it didn't seem like work. We found genuine delight in transforming the clutter into orderly comfort in a cabin we could finally call our own. I shook the curtains and rehung them, washed the fly-specked windows, knocked down sooty cobwebs, peeled pictures from the walls, and nailed back loose paneling. Freda spent the morning emptying the built-in cooler and ramshackle pantry and sorting the contents, neatly restocking the clean shelves.

In the afternoon, with steel wool and stove oil, I scoured the old Wedgewood and wiped it down with rags. When I was done it shone darkly, decidedly handsome. Hot soapy water made the old icebox gleam, and we set it outside to let fresh air finish the job. In a few weeks, we knew, the snowbanks would be gone and we would need it. In fact, the snowbank on the porch had shrunk so much in the heat that I had to dig a new hole for the bucket. To keep food cold in midsummer would mean hauling block ice up the lake from the Chalet.

By the end of the day the cabin was reasonably neat and much cleaner. The unwanted furniture, if totally worthless, had been broken up for stovewood, or neatly stacked against the wall in the parlor. On the front porch, a heap of iron bedframes, bedsprings, and boxes of junk waited to be hauled down the lake to the dump when the channel rose and Upper Granite became accessible by boat.

While Freda fixed dinner I set up my fly rod and went out on the bluff to cast for trout. The sun was going down and a few fish were rising. I was tired but happy. Fly fishing for trout in front of my own cabin was a vivid part of my childhood dream. By the time Freda called me to dinner an hour later I had caught three rainbows of eight or nine inches. I carried them inside with a feeling of deep satisfaction.

The next morning after breakfast, drinking coffee in the sun, we looked up to see Jorgy in the open kitchen doorway intently studying the room. "I can't believe it," he said. "You've got it looking really nice. I wouldn't have thought it was possible." Accepting a mug of coffee and perching on a stool, he told us he'd been convinced the place was past fixing. And that was what he'd told everyone who'd asked his opinion. He was delighted with the change our brief cleaning had made and eager to tell us what we ought to do next.

The first thing, he said, was to buy an old apartment-sized gas range to make the cooking easier for Freda. Most cabins had one, and his boat crews made periodic "flamo" runs to deliver the butane tanks that fueled them. And before long, he assured us, we'd want a few gas lights and perhaps a gas refrigerator.

"And if you're going to have a family," he said with a smile, "you want to think about developing your loft. Let's take a look." We pulled down the ladder and climbed up to look around. Since headroom was nonexistent except squarely beneath the peak of the kitchen roof, I didn't see much to develop.

But Jorgy had another idea. He proposed removing the whole lakeward side of the roof and extending the kitchen wall up from below to make the upstairs into a big dormer room. It would mean a small flat roof but the strong prevailing wind should prevent a dangerous buildup of snow. A porch could be extended above a new pantry for easy outside access from the bluff. He had a couple of builders who could handle the job as long as there was someone around to make decisions. They were booked all that summer but we could have them next June if we wanted.

To make sure the foundations would support a second story we crawled under the house through a hatch beneath the porch. The cabin was supported by handy granite outcroppings, conveniently located old stumps, weathered posts and piles of flat rocks. The wood had rotted and the rocks had slipped and were giving no support.

I had been so intent on obtaining the cabin that it hadn't occurred to me to check the foundation. Now that I saw it I feared the agent had been right: the cabin was on the verge of collapse. But to my amazement, Jorgy was favorably impressed. The cabin's underpinnings, he said, were better than those of most old Granite cabins. He pointed out a rare sign of quality: a subfloor of one-by-twelve sugar pine planking. A day's work, he assured me, would restore the foundation. He casually proposed to jack up the cabin and replace the worst piers with posts on concrete pads before beginning on the loft.

The next thing we needed was running water, he said. Freda vigorously nodded. He recommended pumping from the lake to a storage tank in the loft. But he warned us against adding too many conveniences. People who put in flush toilets, electric generators and other complications gradually stopped coming up to use them. When Granite got too much like the city, it seemed to lose its appeal. He looked around the crude kitchen and smiled. "Of course you won't have to worry about that for a while."

The lake had risen enough with the runoff from snowmelt to open the channel, and he had towed our boat all the way to the cove. We went down to the dock to take a look. It was a twelve-foot, bright-red Wizard with the bow decked over and two seats in the cockpit. Our big white Johnson looked huge on the transom. Jorgy confirmed that it had plenty of power and would probably be all right—once we got used to its quirks. He showed me an extra three-gallon can of gas and a packet of shear pins. When I offered to pay he smiled and said everything would be on our bill. He had opened a Chalet account in our names. "Most lakers charge everything they need in the summer. It's easier for both of us than handling money. And I'm so busy all summer you probably won't get a bill before Thanksgiving."

He cautioned me against driving the boat through the channel. Though he'd made it up safely he knew all the rocks. Since the current was strong we could get down by drifting, fending off the rocks with an oar.

Looking at the logs to which the boat had been tied he asked if we'd thought about building a real pier, one with room for the canoe and rowboat we'd probably want. If we were interested in providing deep water mooring that his taxis could use in the fall, he'd pay half the cost of construction, and his crew would build the pier that fall. We should think it over and let him know before August.

As he climbed in his boat he remembered to tell us a cabin on the channel had partly burned last summer and there was lots of old lumber that would be perfect for our stove. We shouldn't miss the chance because firewood, we would find, on our sparsely timbered side of the lake was very scarce. He waved off our thanks, started his engine and disappeared around a point in Upper Granite.

As soon as he was gone I took our boat out for a run around the lake. When I felt I could control it I returned to the cove to pick up an oar for a trip down the channel. But I didn't mean to drift. Freda decided to walk down and watch. Throttling down the engine as slow as it would go, one hand on the gear shift, I edged into the channel, trying to remember the route the taxi had taken the year before.

The current carried me faster than I wanted, and I had to swerve sharply to miss several rocks, but I made the short passage to Lower Granite without hitting anything. Freda stood clapping by the mouth of the channel. I elaborately wiped the sweat from my forehead and bowed. Coming upstream seemed easier at first, but then the bow caught the current and swung me into a rock. The propeller hit, shearing the pin, and I drifted downstream until I could reach an outstretched branch and pull myself to shore.

Half an hour later, after taking off the prop and changing the pin, I made two round trips through the channel without incident. I felt confident now that I could get from the cabin to the car whenever the need arose. We no longer were dependent on others for our transport.

Returning to the cove, I set about improving the dock. Now that we had a boat of our own I wanted a better place to moor it. Beneath the cabin I found planks, old shutters and the remains of a raft. It only took an hour to assemble a crude four-by-eight-foot platform on the logs that formed our landing. A plank bridge joined it to the grassy flat.

By midafternoon the cabin was closed and everything that could suffer from rain was locked inside. When the boat was packed with what we wanted to take home or deliver to the dump, there was scarcely room for us. Despite the heavy load, I eased the boat safely down the channel under power as Freda hung on grimly, holding her breath. She began to relax when we turned down Lower Granite toward our car at the Chalet two miles away.

The lake's south shore, which three days before had been a solid sheet of snow, now showed numerous patches of bare ground, and the lake itself had risen more than a foot. Spring was rapidly turning into summer. At the Chalet we moored the boat in a sheltered slip and loaded the car for the drive to the city. With the cabin clean, our pockets full of lists and plans for the future, and our own boat waiting at the end of the road, we felt well-pleased with our first short stay in Granite Basin.

* * *

It was nearly a month before we returned, the car loaded this time with provisions for nine days. It was clearly summer now, with no sign of snow. The day was cloudless but windy when we reached the Chalet, and big green waves were rolling down the lake. Six inches of water from snowmelt and rain sloshed in the bottom of our bobbing boat which sat so low in the water that waves were beginning to splash over the stern. Another few days and the weight of the engine would have sunk it.

I bailed it and warmed up the motor while Freda unpacked the car and made a few last-minute purchases at the Chalet's small store. When all our gear was stowed in the boat we started up the lake. Beyond the harbor the waves were larger than I'd imagined and the heavily laden boat rose sluggishly to meet them. No matter how slowly we moved into the wind the oncoming waves broke over our bow and sheets of water soaked us and our belongings. I tried more power in hopes of riding higher but the pounding was terrific and Freda begged me to slow down.

When at last we reached our cove our bagged and boxed provisions were soaked from above and sitting in three inches of water. Freda was so grateful the boat hadn't sunk that she laughed when the bottom fell out of the paper bag she was lifting. These conditions, we were to learn, were not unusual at Granite. Strong winds were common and our neighbors took precautions or expected to get wet. As I carried in the first of our sopping gear I made a mental note never to rely on paper bags again. It was days before the last of our equipment was dry, and some of the food never recovered.

The free firewood sounded well worth examining so I followed the channel until I came to a large heap of partially charred siding, timbers and shingles, still smelling of fire. Pleased to see that I could move it by water, I returned to the cabin for a hammer, saw and boxes, then motored down the channel, beaching the boat not twenty yards from the woodpile.

The best short boards and timbers I stacked inside the boat. When these were gone I began cutting longer pieces short enough to fit. Before long I realized it would take me all day to make one full boatload, so I started to stack long boards up against the deck—one end in the stern, the other high in the air. When the boat was nearly full I filled four cartons with shingles and stacked them on top. Getting the boat off the beach was a job, but at last I slowly chugged out of the channel and up the lake to the cove. Freda heard me coming and came down to the dock to welcome me back.

Proud of my haul, I turned smartly into the cove, forgetting the topheavy weight of my load! The boat slowly rolled and for a moment I thought it was going to capsize, but once my cargo had splashed overboard the boat quickly righted. I looked from Freda's anxious face to the cove full of lumber, and we laughed. After docking the boat I waded out into the harbor to salvage my haul. The boxes of shingles, floating like little ships, were easily lifted from the water but it took me an hour to corral all the lumber, shove it ashore, and stack it to dry against the cliff.

While wading in the cove I had noticed a good deal of litter on the bottom. And I had recently discovered a six-pronged spear with a barb on each prong and a long aluminum handle. Since I was already wet I decided to clean up the harbor with the spear.

That, I assumed, was its purpose. Ten years passed before we learned what it had been. We were sitting one night beside a bonfire on the bluff with friends from a neighboring cabin. When I produced the spear to stir up the coals an old-timer exclaimed, "Why I haven't seen that gig in twenty years! Old Norm harpooned some big browns with that baby."

It seemed that big brown trout, some weighing ten pounds, used to come out of the depths in the fall to spawn on the gravel-bottomed pools in the channel. Like the Indians of the region half a century before, the cabin's former owner had made himself a spear to gig trout while they were trying to mate in shallow water. The thought made me shudder.

The volume of debris in our harbor seemed excessive. It was a year or two before we understood why. Our cove lay directly at the foot of Upper Granite, and the prevailing wind blew straight toward it, funneling in everything that floated. If a fisherman ate an apple anywhere on Upper Granite the discarded core washed up on our shore. If a cardboard box blew off somebody's dock it eventually found its way to us. If a canoe came free of its moorings in the night it could be found in our cove in the morning.

Though this necessitated periodic cleaning and sometimes brought us such unpleasantries as dead rats, bloated fish, beer cans, and soggy watermelon rind, it also yielded oars, life jackets, firewood, planks, rafts, trees knocked down by winter avalanches, sail stays, bailing buckets, life preserver cushions, lengths of rope, fishing floats, boat fenders, buoys, and other useful items. The most valuable of these were quickly reclaimed by their owners—who knew where to look—but for years we never thought of buying paddles, oars, or life preservers.

Toward the end of our stay I took the car and went to see the real estate agent, who also dealt in furniture and plumbing supplies. He had expressed a marked interest in several old pieces, and I hoped we could do a little trading. I told him what we needed and he showed me through several of his sheds and storerooms. An hour later I drove back to the lake with a double boxspring and mattress on the roof and a small gas range and flamo regulator in the trunk.

The agent came to visit the following day and I was pleased to see he had brought a large boat. What he wanted most were the treadle sewing machine, an old rocking chair and a partly dismantled iron stove—none of which we wanted. We agreed to give up the three priceless antiques on the condition that he remove all the rest of our unwanted furniture. He readily accepted and I was glad to help him carry it all down to his boat. He left heavily loaded but happy. We were even more delighted. Everything we'd wanted to get rid of was gone and our bed, stove, and plumbing hadn't cost us a penny. Suddenly the cabin seemed twice as large and far more cheerful. Now we could begin to think of other changes. On our way to the city we stopped at the Chalet and ordered our first tank of flamo from Jorgy.

* * *

When we next came to Granite, in the middle of August, we brought with us a six week old St. Bernard puppy named Rafferty. He was so clumsy and small he couldn't climb the steps and had to be carried almost everywhere we went. If left alone for more than a minute he began a piteous crying. We put our old mattress in a hollow on the ledge overlooking the lake, and there he contentedly dozed in the sun, especially if someone kept him company.

The first project that trip was to hook the new stove to the two-hundred-pound flamo tank Jorgy's crew had delivered. We propped the tank against the back of the pantry, and I bored one-inch holes through the wall to the kitchen and pantry. Since this installation was temporary, I used flexible plastic tubing in place of galvanized pipe. It bent nicely around corners and fastened neatly with screw clamps and glue. The pressure regulator mounted easily on top of the tank, and the stove was working in time for dinner that night.

Though the breeze from our open front door sometimes blew out the burners and the oven often started with a pop, Freda was delighted. Cooking at a mile and a half above sea level, without benefit of running water or a sink that drained, was trouble enough without having to deal with flaming gasoline spurting from the camp stove or the half-hot-half-not oven of the Wedgewood. No longer would our dinners be cold on one side and charred on the other!

The most dramatic event that August week was the premature demise of the big white outboard. Curious about our purchase, my mother had come to have a look at the cabin. Though she was leery of boats, on her last afternoon she allowed me to persuade her to come for a ride on Upper Granite. We were skimming down the lake, when a faster boat passed us leaving a wake that violently rocked us from side to side. All at once the roar of the motor grew louder and the pitch began to climb. I turned and to my horror saw that one of the clamps that held the motor in place had come loose. The whirling prop was out of water and rising steadily higher.

I made a quick stab at the throttle and missed, then leaped toward the bow, nearly landing on my mother, as the motor jerked free. It seemed to hang for an instant upside down above the boat before plunging with a splash into the lake. Suddenly it was quiet. My mother sat white-faced and still in the bow, watching smoky bubbles rise from the depths.

It was easy enough to see what had happened. The steel plate on the transom had grown slippery from oil oozing out of the engine. When the passing boat's wake had started us rocking the thrust had been sufficient to slide one engine mount free. The second one never had a chance. It had acted as a pivot, permitting the engine to turn in a circle and rip itself loose. We were lucky it had landed in the water, not the boat!

That afternoon I walked down to the channel, hitched a ride to the Chalet, and told Jorgy what had happened. He smiled, reminding me of his warning when he'd delivered the boat that its transom plate needed a lip on top. He had a fourteen-horse Evinrude he'd rent cheaply for the remaining week of the season, giving us all winter to find ourselves a new motor. I accepted his offer and hitched a ride home. Before the Evinrude arrived the following morning the treacherous steel plate on the transom was gone.

Jorgy's proposal for a deep water pier had intrigued us. After a good deal of thought we decided we would need it. We wanted a canoe, several kayaks and a rowboat, and someday I hoped to have a small sailboat. Besides needing moorage we needed some protection from the wind-driven surf that crashed into the cove. When Jorgy brought the motor we set about planning a pier that would follow the south shore of the cove, then dogleg halfway across its mouth to an underwater rock. It would accommodate four boats, function as a breakwater, and give Jorgy a low-water berth in the fall. And between the pier and the rock that flanked the cove was a sheltered space I could deck over and put to good use.

It was a large undertaking, but since Jorgy was anxious to build that fall and willing to absorb half the cost, we decided to go ahead—especially when he told us we could take until the following summer to pay. Since it was then late August, there was no time to lose. Although work on the foundations could not begin until the lake reached low water in mid-September, all materials had to be delivered well beforehand. Once Labor Day arrived and the spillway was opened the channel would be too shallow for taxis within a week. Once the water was down anything forgotten would have to be carried from Lower Granite on someone's back.

Jorgy made drawings and a material list, and very soon thereafter passing Chalet boats began to make deliveries. One brought a wheelbarrow, another reinforcing rod, a third a portable generator. Then the workboat arrived with planking and timbers and ninety-pound sacks of cement. The sand, we were told, would be hauled from the beach that emerged in Cornell Cove when the water dropped.

That final week in August used the last of our vacation, but we planned to come back some weekend in the fall to watch construction and close the cabin for the winter. This time when we docked the boat at the Chalet, we let Jorgy store it in his boatbarn for the winter.

* * *

It was early October before we got back to the basin again. The day was cold and the sun shone dimly through a threatening haze. Smoke was rising from the chimney of the Chalet and inside we found Jorgy at work on his books. By the time he came to join us at the fire it was snowing. For an hour we talked, watching the swirling snow above the harbor through the window. Then it stopped and seemed to be clearing.

A boy who had driven Chalet boats all summer appeared and offered to take us up the lake. After making arrangements with Jorgy to be picked up the following afternoon, we carried our food box and old kerosene heater out the snow-covered pier to the boat. Rafferty frisked in the miniature snowbanks, licking and barking and rolling in the drifts. The lake was down five feet and Freda, now six months pregnant, had a hard time climbing down the slippery iron ladder to the boat. When I handed down Rafferty—fifty pounds of flopping legs and loose skin—he nearly knocked the boat boy in the lake.

We had hardly cleared the harbor when it began to snow again. Halfway up the lake the wind began to blow and mists closed in around us, blocking our view of the shore. It was bitterly cold and I helped Freda crawl beneath the deck in the bow where Raff had already taken refuge. The wind raised a swell and it began to get rough. With the shore lost in mist and swirling snow it was hard to gauge our location. The boy looked worried. "I'm gonna turn back," he yelled at me, "I'm lost."

I told him I thought he ought to go on because we had to be close to the lake's upper end. He hesitated, anxious, then panicked. "Here, you take it," he said, and dove beneath the deck to join Freda and Raff. I grabbed the wheel and tried to keep the same course, guided solely by the wind, which I assumed was still blowing down the middle of the basin. At this end of the lake when the water was down I knew there were rocks well out from shore, and I strained to see them through the wind-driven snow, my unprotected face and hands turning numb.

All at once Freda cried that water was pouring in on top of them. It didn't seem possible but I crouched down for a look. Incredibly enough there was a hole in the bow the size of my fist, and the boy's extra weight had put it underwater. I ordered him out and he reluctantly crawled to the stern, which stopped the leak. I turned back to our course just in time to see rocks in the water straight ahead. Swinging the wheel hard, I prayed for the prop. We hit a rock and bounced off but luckily the pin did not shear. I slowed to a crawl, and in less than a minute the dark shape of the boathouse appeared in the mist.

By the time we reached it, the snow had stopped falling and the mist was clearing fast. I invited the boy to come warm up at the cabin and drink a cup of tea, but the lake was almost clear now—we could see the Chalet—and he was anxious to start back before the mist closed in again. I picked up the heater while Freda took the food box, and we made our way through the snow to the cabin, Raff frolicking happily in the drifts.

An hour later we were warm and dry, and eating hot apple pie by the stove in our fast-warming kitchen. Outside the sky had cleared and the snow-dusted basin was brilliant in the sunshine. Our breath made clouds of steam in the freezing air. In the flat by the cove stacks of lumber and sacks of cement were only mounds in the snow. Out in the cove the skeleton of our new pier was nearly complete. Another day of good weather and the hard part would be done. The decking could be nailed on in the spring.

Jorgy came to get us the next afternoon. A strong breeze was blowing and the water was getting rough. As we sped down the lake a white sky began to lower, and before we reached our car it was snowing again. Our first summer at the cabin was over.

THREE

Rebuilding the Cabin

Since the cabin, when we bought it, wasn't thought worth repairing, it obviously needed a good deal of work. Maybe more than we could manage. But it didn't take us long, once the cabin was cleaned out, to develop an affection for the ruin we had bought, or to see ways to restore and even modestly improve it.

The cabin may have been decrepit, but it was certainly authentic. Age had conferred a certain richness and warmth that could never be reproduced in something new. It looked, felt, smelled, and behaved as a mountain cabin should. Though anything but handsome, it harmonized well with its wilderness surroundings. The word "cabin" makes me think of weathered, seasoned wood well-scarred with years of use. Our cabin had that look, and the look had been honestly acquired. Its wind-etched thin shakes could not be replaced. Few men know how to split them anymore, and the trees from which shake blocks were cut are nearly gone.

We loved the big square kitchen and ramshackle pantry for their water-stained walls, smoky beams and sun-bleached sills. The south-tilting floor testified to the settling induced by the stream, and the antiquated plate rail made a handy shelf for books and driftwood, pinecones, and rocks. The mellow, battered paneling that lined both rooms, we learned years later, had been salvaged from the superintendent's office of a burned-out gold rush lumbermill. This explained why, when we remod-

32

eled, we found some of it was charred on the back. That paneling was already a hundred years old when we arrived.

By the end of our first summer, difficult as it had been, we wouldn't have considered tearing down the cabin—even if we had had the money to build a new one, which we didn't. So repairs would have to be inexpensive.

We had three main areas of need. We needed to strengthen and reinforce the cabin structurally so it would withstand the wind and heavy snows. We needed to chink its many cracks to keep out wind, snow, water, and wildlife. And we needed more sleeping room, storage, plumbing and heating.

Since Freda, as cook, would be the most burdened by primitive conditions, I felt an obligation to provide better kitchen facilities. She deserved a good stove, a counter, and running water. Gas and kerosene lanterns would do for light, and the outhouse up the hill presented no problem, but I hoped for a fireplace and the luxury of hot showers.

That first summer we discovered we had a particularly windy location. The slightest wind on a chilly day made the cabin impossible to heat. The drafts were so strong they rattled the loose windows, billowed the curtains, and sent dustdevils dancing across the floor. And when the wind was blowing hard the cabin trembled and shook, creaking and bending in every strong gust, as though daring us to doubt that it could easily collapse.

Apparently the cabin had been built in two stages, and never structurally united. The rooms not only gave each other no support, they moved independently in the wind. From the loft I could look down through the gap between the walls and see the rocks beneath the cabin. When the wind was blowing hard the gap opened and closed and the walls sawed back and forth in a disconcerting manner.

After a summer at the cabin we were ready to go ahead with Jorgy's suggestion for developing the loft. By removing half the lakeside roof above both rooms, then extending the walls up to second-story height, we would gain a large area for sleeping and storage, while uniting the cabin into a single structural unit. Not only would we get the sleeping loft I'd always wanted, we'd gain

33

a second-story porch overlooking the lake—at a minimal cost for the added floorspace.

When we told Jorgy we were prepared to go ahead, he took pains to explain—perhaps warn would be more accurate—that building at Granite was nothing like building in the city. First there were the builders: Bat and Slim. You couldn't call them carpenters because they couldn't read plans, but what they built would stand up against the wind and snow. Whether they built what you wanted, of course depended on how well you could communicate your hopes—and how well Bat and Slim liked your plans!

Then there was the matter of the cabin itself. Nothing in it was straight or square or plumb. Trying to add on would drive a conscientious carpenter crazy. But Bat and Slim would not be fazed by the mare's nest of box ends that made up our loft. They were good at making do and always ready to compromise in the face of adversity. If what they built was less than perfect, what could we expect, considering what we'd given them to work with?

It was essential that I be on hand to make suggestions and decisions, and I really ought to plan to help out on the job if we wanted to keep down the cost. If Bat and Slim were left on their own there was no telling what they might build—maybe nothing. If we could live in the cabin while the job was going on, and if the ice went out by the first week in June, we could have Jorgy's builders for the week or two we'd need them.

We were anxious to start and immediately agreed. Jorgy said he'd order enough lumber to get the job rolling and try to explain things to Bat and Slim beforehand. There wasn't any use to try to make plans. Once the roof was torn off we'd put our heads together and figure out what to do next. Bat and Slim were sure to have some ideas of their own. He'd come around now and then to see how things were going, but the rest of the time it would be up to me to keep the job going.

We set the starting date for a Monday in the middle of June, and came up the Saturday before to get ready. The weather was fair when we arrived but on Sunday it turned cloudy and the wind began to blow. We kept busy and warm clearing workspace and spreading enormous drop cloths across the porous loft floor.

Jorgy arrived after lunch, heavily dressed against the cold, with a load of shingles, lumber, building paper and sacked cement. We helped him unload and wrap the cement in plastic tarps, and in late afternoon it started to rain. Just before dark the rain turned to hail and then stopped. At bedtime the night seemed so ominously quiet that I went outside to check. It was snowing.

We awoke on Monday to the gloomiest of mornings. Four inches of new snow blanketed the ground, and a wet heavy fog hung just above the water. It was damp and cold and utterly still, and we couldn't believe that anyone would come. Then we heard a motor and I ran to the window to see the old barge emerge from the channel and turn our way. I jumped into my clothes and went down to meet it at the dock.

The dour Slim sat silent and muffled in the bow, expressing himself with periodic spurts of tobacco juice. Bat, small and wiry and as talkative as his partner was quiet, jumped out, shivering, and gave the sky a worried look. "She looks pretty bad, but Jorgy said to come up and see if you wanted your roof torn off today."

The thought was unnerving, but I couldn't very well send them away. They might never come back! So I tried to grin and said, "Sure, go ahead."

An hour later the fog disappeared and strong June sunlight poured down on the job. Well before noon half the roof above both rooms was gone, leaving an open loft that looked like the stage in a rustic little theatre. Jorgy's arrival, like the change in the weather, was perfectly timed, and the four of us set about deciding what to do next.

Bat wanted a pitched roof that would put me on my knees every time I wanted to look out the windows, while Slim called for an expensive row of dormer windows. Jorgy listened politely then offered his solution: a single dormer room with good head-room and a nearly flat roof. He felt we could get by with very little pitch because the span was short and the wind down the lake would keep snow from building up. I said I was willing to risk it.

"All right," said Slim gloomily, "if that's what you want. But don't come to me when she smashes flat."

Next Jorgy explained the need to frame the room in a way that would tie the two sections of the cabin together. He made the job a challenge, scornfully pointing out how poorly the original builders had done, and expressing boundless confidence in Bat and Slim's ability to make the cabin strong. Then he quickly left, motioning me to follow. Down on the dock he told me it was best to leave them alone once they knew what had to be done. They didn't want or need supervision.

By quitting time, with the weather warm and the snow nearly gone, the header and frame for the two new walls were up, and half the new rafters in place. It was hard to believe so much had been accomplished after such an unpromising start, and I was whistling as I sorted the heap of debris that had been the roof.

The next day Bat and Slim brought a helper named Gregg, and there very soon developed a rivalry between them for his services. There was a good deal of arguing and not much was getting done, until I joined the crew as second helper. I worked

36

with old Slim, who devised a clever brace and tie arrangement for uniting the two buildings effectively.

Bat, in the meantime, had come to the conclusion that patching the old north wall was a mistake. To Slim's annoyance, he called me over. It would be easier, he thought, to rip off the old shakes clear down to the porch and reface. And while the wall was open I ought to replace the kitchen windows and door. I told him I had planned to replace them sometime later, when there wasn't so much to do.

"Hell, why wait?" he protested. "Order all your windows now and put 'em in while everything's torn up. That's the way to save money and mess."

I was easily persuaded to add three big windows to the list, and Bat thought he knew of a good used door he could get "for a dollar or two." After lunch Gregg and I were sent to the roof to cover the rafters with pine planking, while Bat and Slim worked amiably together to complete the studding and the tie between the two buildings. It was marvelous up there in the sun on the roof, drinking cold beer, driving nails and watching the big sailing cumulus clouds, while from beneath came the comforting sounds of hammer and saw and murmuring voices. The job, for the moment at least, was running smoothly, and summer seemed to have arrived.

Wednesday began with a quick razing of the pantry, which came away from the kitchen in one piece. Gregg and I dragged it to the firepit, doused it with kerosene and set it afire. The tinder-dry wood burned fiercely to ashes in less than ten minutes. "That'll give you some idea of how your cabin would go if she ever caught fire," Bat observed.

Jorgy had prescribed new foundations for the kitchen wall, which had now doubled in weight, so at eight locations selected by Slim, we dug holes beneath the wall and filled them with concrete. The procedure was the same at support points for the future porch and pantry. In the afternoon Bat and Slim teamed up to join the old roof to the new. Fitting new shingles among the old proved exasperating work, and I pretended not to hear their threats and complaints.

Every day at five o'clock, when the crew climbed back in the barge and chugged away, Freda and I began the day's cleanup.

We filled carton after carton with wood scraps that would fit in the stove. New lumber was restacked, concrete bags were burned and nails were pulled from reusable boards. Pieces of the roof, which would one day be firewood, we dragged well away from the job site and piled. When the loft and woodpiles were reasonably neat, we put away the tools and swept out the dust that had filtered through the ceiling to the kitchen below. Then we were ready for dinner, and the rest of the evening could be devoted to luxurious indolence.

On Thursday Slim decided the concrete had cured and he lifted the cabin with a twenty-ton screw jack so Bat could install support posts on the new foundations. Supports were also built for the loft-level porch and the pantry that in time would sit beneath it.

After lunch, Jorgy arrived with a boatload of windows, and we carried them up to the loft. Bat was so sure they were going to get broken that he kept after Slim until the older man agreed to help install them that afternoon. At the end of the day the loft was a room with windows and a roof, but no walls.

Friday was my final day on the job. Bat and Slim would not be back until Monday, and by then we'd be gone. The room was closed in a little after lunch, and almost immediately it started to rain. How thoughtful, said Freda, of the storm to wait until we're ready! The weather drove us inside where we discussed the work to be completed the following week—flooring the loft, installing the kitchen windows, hanging new doors both downstairs and up, and building an inside stairway to replace the flimsy ladder to the loft.

When the rain settled down to an unpleasant drizzle Bat and Slim became engrossed in planning the stairway, heatedly arguing for nearly an hour before reaching agreement just as quitting time arrived. With considerable relief we watched them sail away. After five long days we looked forward to the privacy and peace of the weekend.

On Sunday afternoon, after cleaning up the cabin and grounds one last time, we were finally ready to leave. As I began to load the boat under darkening skies it started to rain. I covered our things with a tarp and went inside. Within minutes it was pouring and lightning was stabbing from the mass of black clouds that hid the basin. Freda and our baby daughter, Katherine, lay down on the big bed and promptly went to sleep. I stretched out on the couch to listen to the thunder, certain the storm would let up shortly.

An hour later I awoke, feeling marvelously refreshed. Bright sunlight was streaming in the window. While Freda made coffee and heated the last of a cinnamon coffee cake, I bailed two inches of water from the stern of the boat and finished loading. Steam was rising from the surface of the water as we made our way down Lower Granite to the car.

When we returned to the cabin the following weekend big aluminum sash windows and a new Dutch door had transformed the dark kitchen into a light and cheerful room with marvelous views. A steep but functional staircase led up to the bright and spacious loft which was actually two rooms on slightly different levels. The smaller, tucked under the eaves, would be Kath's bedroom, while we moved our bed to the huge unfinished gallery just above. A door opened out to a deck overlooking the lake, from which three steps conveniently led down to the bluff.

In two weeks' time, thanks to Bat and Slim and Jorgy, we had accomplished far more than originally planned, but when I made a list of what remained to be done, I realized the job was just beginning. Since Bat and Slim were gone for good, most of the work would be mine. First I finished up the pantry to make it ready for the old Servel gas refrigerator we had bought the winter before.

After hauling fifty pound blocks of ice up the lake in the bottom of the boat for our rusty and inefficient tin icebox, we looked forward to real refrigeration. Jorgy's crew brought the little fridge up the lake on a flamo run, set it in place in the pantry, and helped me hook it to the temporary gas line. I changed the orifice to handle flamo, made the prescribed high-altitude adjustment, filled the ice tray with water, and lighted the gas burner that was somehow supposed to make everything cold. The next morning we had ice. We also had frozen milk, frozen meat and frozen lettuce. The little fridge was so efficient we had to turn it down to "defrost" to keep it from functioning as a freezer.

The last thing I built that summer was a "mouse closet."

Every cabin in the basin needed one mouse-proof place to store bedding and linen for the winter. A determined mouse, with all winter to work, can gnaw his way through two or three inches of wood. The mouse closet I built in the space beneath the stairs was far from impregnable, but only twice have mice succeeded in chewing their way inside, and the damage was slight.

The following summer, on a day of heavy wind, a Chalet boat pulled up to let off a county building inspector, perhaps the first to visit the basin. His superiors had sent him to inspect our new loft. He looked worried, slightly seasick, and walked through the loft without comment. When I pressed him for a comment he said that everything looked fine, but was I sure we could make it safely back down the lake in this weather?

It was a rough wet ride, even by Granite standards, and he was greatly relieved when I put him ashore. He assured me the county approved everything I'd built. He must have told his colleagues about the harrowing trip, because inspectors remained scarce for some years thereafter!

Our greatest needs, with the loft complete, were to plumb the cabin for water and gas, improve Freda's kitchen, and provide a better method of heating. Since these needs were all related, it made sense to devise a comprehensive plan.

Hot and cold running water was our biggest problem, so I tackled it first. To get gravity flow to a shower downstairs meant a water heater in the loft. That, in turn, meant a tank on the nearly flat roof, to be supplied by a pump on the lakeshore. With our water source planned, I turned my attention to plumbing the inside of the cabin.

But before any piping could be installed, I discovered, we needed a new sink equipped with faucets and a drain. Before a sink could be installed, there had to be a counter and cabinets beneath to support it. Before installing cabinets we needed to know how much space would be required by the new stove Freda wanted. With priorities established I turned to the matter of replacing the old wood-burning Wedgewood. Of course replacing the stove meant replacing its heating capacity as well.

With all winter to shop I was able to find the perfect stove. It, too, was a Wedgewood, but powered by gas, with an oven, broiler, four burners and a skillet on top. But what made it ideal was

40

the built-in 20,000 BTU gas heater on one side. Before it arrived we had to plumb the cabin permanently for gas. That meant moving the flamo tank so it wouldn't interfere with our view across the lake. The only way to get it completely out of sight was to hide it behind the outhouse. Since galvanized pipe was just as ugly as the tank, we decided to run it underground, which meant digging some fifty feet of trench through almost solid rock.

When the trench was ready, after three days' work, the actual plumbing was relatively simple. Included in the job were three gaslights: one for the stove, one in the pantry and the third above a desk in the parlor.

Getting the new Wedgewood to the cabin wasn't easy since it weighed in the neighborhood of three hundred pounds. Even stripped and dismantled it took four of us to carry it from the trailer to the boat, and then we had to make a detour because we couldn't squeeze it between the trees. But once the stove was inside, hookup with a flexible connection was simple, and that night Freda cooked a banquet to celebrate. We missed the crackle and the smoky scent of burning wood, but the new stove took a lot of the work out of cooking, and we marveled at its ability to heat the kitchen.

With the new stove in place it was easy to position the cabinets and install ten feet of countertop and a new stainless steel sink. Freda was delighted. With storage, counters, a good stove, a cold fridge, gas lights and instant heat, all her kitchen lacked was hot and cold running water.

After considerable figuring I devised what I thought was a neat and simple plan for piping the cabin. When I showed it to Jorgy, not without pride, he innocently smiled and said "Can't water run both up a pipe and down?" He took my pencil and scratched out half my piping, added a vent, a pressure relief valve for the water heater, repositioned all piping so it would quickly drain through two strategically located hose bibs, and added shutoff and foot valves to keep the water from running back into the lake. Then he handed back the plan, and said it looked very good!

The continual remodeling of those early years meant numerous boat trips down the lake for supplies. At the Chalet dock one

Saturday morning I was about to shove off with a well-laden boat when a stranger walked up and asked if it was true that there were cabins beyond the road. When I confirmed the fact, he said, almost with alarm, "Then everything past here must be carried in by boat. Why, that must mean thousands of trips!"

It was true. Since hauling things out was just as much trouble as hauling them in most cabinowners keep a private store of building materials and tools. It never hurt to inquire among one's friends before making a trip down the lake for one small item. So, before I went outside to shop for plumbing supplies, I walked around to talk to my neighbors. A community water system just up the hill had been recently dismantled and I found a large supply of slightly bent galvanized pipe that the owners were eager to sell for five cents a foot. I carried all I needed to the cabin in less than an hour.

Along the way I learned quite by chance that one of my neighbors owned a new twenty-gallon water heater that had never been hooked up. Though slightly dented, it had a high recovery rating, was designed for high altitude, and equipped for bottled gas. He was willing to sell it for twenty dollars and helped me carry it down the trail to my cabin. It was exactly what we needed and it fit very neatly beneath the eaves behind Kath's bed. She called it "the General" (from the brand name on the side), and in the years to come its cozy warmth, soft bubbling, and flickering light became a comfort in the night.

Downstairs, directly underneath the General in which had once been a closet, I assembled and then enclosed a stall shower. By knocking out two walls and reapportioning the space, I was able to construct a shower room and a combination tool room and closet beside the loft stairs. The shower room, hidden from the parlor by a curtain, offered a place to dress, a counter, a medicine cabinet and a view of Talking Mountain through a window that also let out the steam.

The job produced a pair of surprises. I had just driven a nail in an interior wall when I heard a quiet hissing and began to smell gas. It seemed utterly impossible, but when I pried back the paneling I found a neatly punctured copper gasline that had been cleverly concealed when the gaslight was hung in the parlor. I shut off the valve at the flamo tank and, having no fittings, simply filled the hole with a drop of epoxy, a makeshift repair that still serves. Not half an hour later I was nailing on trim outside the shower room window when again I heard hissing—this time much louder. Another gasline seemed impossible, but I leaned close to sniff. It certainly wasn't butane! Hurrying inside, I opened the medicine cabinet to find my nail stuck into a bubbling aerosol can of mosquito repellent. The odor lasted a week, but the area stayed free of mosquitos.

At the foot of the stairs the view was superb, but the old wooden window was small and too high, so I decided to replace it with a new window, five feet high. I installed it in a hurry one Saturday morning, with the help of a friend who had only the weekend to visit. The weather was warm and we were anxious to go swimming, so we hastily sawed the hole, built a frame, and nailed in the new sash. Then we went outside to take a look.

To our astonishment we discovered the window leaned ten degrees! But when we came back inside it again seemed perfectly vertical. I put a level on the floor, and sure enough, it tilted. And so did everything else in the room, making the window look perfectly plumb. By cheating a little with the framing outside we managed to disguise about half the window's lean, but when we quit to go swimming I had a greater understanding of Bat and Slim's problems.

When all the necessary appliances—sink, shower, and water heater—were finally in place and the pipe was on the job, I notified Jorgy and he arrived to finish the plumbing. To complete the job we needed a sump to handle water from the shower and sink. Deciding where to dig it was easy. There was only one spot, well back from the lake, that was lower than the floor and contained enough soil for percolation. A friend and I spent most of two days digging a hundred-gallon hole among the spreading roots of two big pines. Two solid-core doors formed a roof which we covered with several inches of dirt. Ten years have passed and it hasn't caved in yet.

That winter I bought a portable pump, powered by a one-cylinder gas engine, for sixty dollars and a slightly dented eighty-two gallon water tank for thirty. A sculptor friend welded a footing to the tank and drilled it for bolts. When the ice was gone the following June we arrived at the lake with tank and pump crammed in the back of our station wagon, along with Kath and Raff. Several curious neighbors, who were sure we were building a solar heating system, helped lift the tank to the roof. The pump was set on a shelf of rock by the lake, and Jorgy made the hookups with black plastic pipe.

When all the valves were open, we primed the pump with a teakettle full of water and fired up the gasoline engine. Jorgy made adjustments until the engine ran smoothly, and gradually the pipe grew cold beneath our hands. We ran indoors and opened all the faucets. At first they only belched air, but rusty water soon followed, and finally the flow was smooth and clear. Freda put her hands in the stream and sighed, "At last!"

I climbed the ladder to the roof and felt the rising level of cold in the tank. The roof seemed rigid and strong, but the tank when filled would weigh nine hundred pounds! There wasn't any bracing directly underneath so it was easy to imagine the roof collapsing. It was too late now to worry, but I called down to Kath and Freda to keep clear, and I moved to the end of the roof to wait. Five minutes passed, then all at once a jet of water shot from the tank's overflow and I waved to Jorgy to shut off the pump. So far the roof had held, but how strong was it now? I had to know. I walked up to the tank, adding my hundred and sixty pounds to its burden. Still nothing happened. I walked around the tank, and finally jumped up and down beside it. The roof seemed absolutely rigid. Bat and Slim had done their job well.

With considerable relief I climbed down to the loft and fired up the water heater, while Jorgy tightened fittings to stop a couple of leaks.

That evening after dinner, by the light of a lantern, Freda enjoyed the luxury of washing dishes in hot and cold running water. Later in the evening I stepped into the candlelit shower for a long and happy soak. There was just enough pressure for steady gentle flow from the big brass flowerpot showerhead.

It's impossible to convey the deep satisfaction we felt that night after spending several summers dipping water from the lake in all kinds of weather, hauling it by bucket up a path to the cabin, then heating it in a teakettle on a woodburning stove everytime a dish or a face needed washing.

With the advent of running water our daily consumption jumped from less than ten gallons to something over fifty, which meant the pump must be run every day. With so much pumping required, we quickly developed a routine. I would start the engine and return to whatever I was doing. Inside the cabin Freda and Kath would listen for the sound of overflow water pouring on the roof. The first to hear it would shout "It's raining!" so I could shut down the engine before the path beneath the eaves turned to mud. Of course we never quite knew when the tank would suddenly run dry, and more than once, in the middle of my shower on a stormy night, when I was well-covered with lather, the shower would trickle and die. Then I would have to beg Freda to try to crank up the engine by flashlight. If she couldn't I'd have to go start it myself.

At first the system worked perfectly, then one fall the pump froze, and the time required to fill the tank rose from five minutes to eight, then twelve and finally twenty-two! In the meantime a new community water system had succeeded in developing a spring on Star Peak and installing a pipeline that came within three hundred feet of the cabin. So instead of replacing the pump, we joined. Laying the connecting pipeline was easy. Mike and I managed to dig the needed trench and bury all the plastic pipe in one day. Not only was it simple to bend the plastic around rocks, it never needed to be drained because it stretched just enough to accommodate the expansion of freezing water.

With the loft developed, the kitchen remodeled, and the cabin plumbed for gas and running water, only the parlor remained to be developed. We needed more sleeping space, storage, and light. All our needs, I decided, could be effectively met by extending the room with a glassed-in bay that would accommodate a built-in windowseat-bed.

A carpenter erected the framework, built a shed roof and installed the glass. I had just enough salvaged shakes to cover the new siding with a properly weathered exterior. The bunk inside had hinged plywood lids providing access to closet-sized storage. Freda liked it so well she prevailed on me to build its twin against the opposite wall. Both were faced with the ancient lumbermill paneling and fitted with thick foam mattresses covered with canvas.

All that remained to complete the parlor—and the cabin—was a fieldstone fireplace in the middle of the wall between the two bunks. Jorgy assured me that Bat was an accomplished stonemason and sent him around to look at the site and advise me. The location I had in mind would mean a tall chimney, but Bat agreed "it would look kinda funny" to build it anywhere else. At least there was solid rock just below the floor. The fireplace, he insisted, should be built around a double-walled steel firebox, complete with smoke shelf, damper and patented throat. "It's the only way to be sure she'll draw. Half the fireplaces in this basin just eat up wood and give no heat. And the other half only give you smoke." He shook his head in disgust.

My job, he said, besides getting the two hundred pound firebox to the cabin, was to stockpile rock and sand for the job. But all my attempts to get some idea of quantity were met with frustration.

"You wouldn't believe how much rock she's gonna take," he said gravely. "You can't get too much. The more I got to choose from the quicker she'll go up." When I asked about sand he said "Get me a couple good piles, knee high, maybe higher. We don't wanna stop to haul sand. No, sir!" Then he showed me the various sizes of rocks that would be needed, urging me to "get as many square ones as you can. The more flat sides, the better they build."

Scouting the area, I found two rock slides within a hundred yards of the cabin that would yield all the rock he could possibly need. I borrowed a big balloon-tired wheelbarrow, then with a pick and shovel I built a barrow road from the job site to both slides. Finally, I hired a neighbor's son, Don, to haul rock. I would pick my way through a rockslide, select good-looking specimens and roll or throw them downhill to the barrow road. Don would load them into the wheelbarrow and wheel it to the cabin. After three exhausting days the slope behind the fireplace site was heaped with tons of individually selected rocks, enough, I felt sure, to build half a dozen fireplaces.

Then we went to work gathering sand. After filling the open

cockpit of the motorboat with all the pails, buckets, basins and tubs we could find, we chugged across the lake to Cornell Cove, which is floored in lovely white granite sand. Unfortunately, all of it is underwater in the summer. Standing thigh-deep in water, we would lift a shovelful of sand from the bottom, let the water drain away, and empty it into a bucket in the boat. When all the containers were full we headed home.

Back at the dock we emptied the sand into the wheelbarrow and pushed it up the path to the cabin, where we dumped it onto an old canvas tarp. After four afternoons I hoped we had enough. There was a rounded pile three feet high and eight feet across, oozing a steady stream of water. To keep the sand from washing away in the spring thaw, we covered the pile with several sheets of plastic anchored with big rocks.

The double-walled steel firebox I brought up from the city in the back of the stationwagon. It took four of us to get it out of the car and into the boat for the trip up the lake, but eventually it reached the cabin, where we stowed it under canvas for the winter.

The following summer, once the sandpile and rocks were free of snow, I notified Jorgy I was ready for Bat. First, he explained, we had to find someone with a strong back and a weak mind to act as his helper. Bat had to have a continuous supply of rock and mixed mortar handy. I asked how long construction should take. When Jorgy guessed three days, I said I'd take the job. Bat and I got along, and I thought my back would hold up for three days. The boss showed up a few days later to figure materials and see what I had gathered. He approved my selection of rock with a grunt, told me to bring in "a leetle more sand," and said he'd be back two days later to begin.

Within an hour of his arrival on construction day I was mixing concrete to his demanding specifications. "Go easy on the water. She wants to be stiff for your foundation, you know. Too sloppy and she won't take the weight." I mixed batch after batch, my back and arms aching, and wheeled them to the site of the six foot square foundation, where Bat would quickly dump the barrow and call for "more mud!" By lunchtime the slab had reached the level of the floor, and by mid-afternoon it was

47

sufficiently set to allow us to gently set the firebox in place. Gradually the facing of field stone grew higher, and by quitting time it hid the firebox completely.

The next morning Bat threw together a skimpy scaffold that supported two stout planks six feet above the ground. He climbed nimbly to his platform, balanced his mortarboard on a section of flue and called for mortar "just a leetle bit sloppy 'cause she's gonna be hot." My job that day, besides shoveling up fresh mortar without upsetting the precariously balanced boards was to hand up terra cotta chimney flue and keep the platform stocked with rocks of various sizes. No matter how fast I moved I was always behind with either mortar or rocks, and Bat would finally take pity and hop down to help his laboring but unpracticed assistant.

We began the third day by moving the staging higher, to twelve feet above the ground. Two ladders were lashed in place for access and support, and a pulley was rigged from the highest rung so I could haul up mortar or rock in a bucket. When Bat moved above the pulley to the peak of the roof I had to carry each bucket of concrete up the ladder and lift it above my head so he could reach it. It was back-breaking work, but exhilarating, too, and when the final row of rocks was in place and topped off, I was almost sorry we were finished.

It was a pleasure the next morning to sit back comfortably in the parlor and watch Bat build a facing of our handsomest rock around the mouth of the firebox. When the grilles that were to circulate the air were in place, he floored the ashpit with firebrick and laid a flagstone hearth. Then I helped him set the massive redwood mantle in place, and we were done.

The last of our original projects was complete.

The cabin was developed and restored as we wished. We had everything we wanted and nothing we didn't. Our little house was strong and relatively tight, comfortable to live in no matter what the weather. There was space and light, shelter and heat, a decent kitchen, good beds, and the luxury—in summer, at least —of hot showers.

But the qualities we wanted to preserve are still intact. The old paneling remains, smoky beams still roof the kitchen and the battered green floor still tilts to the south. Mouse nests insulate the walls, some of them still inhabited, and at night the cabin glows with the soft yellow flames of gaslights and candles.

Though we proved the cabin didn't need to be torn down, Jorgy and the agent were right in one sense: repairs *were* more trouble than starting from scratch. It took us six years to rebuild and develop! But we don't regret our choice—now that all the work is finally done.

FOUR

On Winter Patrol

During the winter Jorgy patrolled the snow-filled basin on skis to safeguard the cabins from hazards such as fallen trees, broken windows, blown-open doors, invasion by animals, dangerous snow loads, avalanche damage, and break-ins by unwanted guests. Every few weeks, between big storms, he skied up the road from the highway to his cabin overlooking the Chalet. From there, depending on the weather, he would ski along the margins of the ice-covered lakes and inspect all the cabins that subscribed to his services.

He told me how peaceful Granite was in the winter, how utterly different everything looked when the frozen lakes were deeply buried under snow. And he asked if I would like to come along. I told him an automobile accident had kept me off skis for almost ten years, but I'd like to try. He promised to give me a call sometime that winter, and in February he did. There had been an unusually heavy storm and he was anxious to see how the cabins had fared before another storm blew in. He'd be glad to have some company if I cared to come along.

His cabin at the foot of Lower Granite was as far as I needed to go, but I was welcome to accompany him on a tour of the basin if I wanted. He had an old pair of army surplus skis I could use, so all I needed were my clothes, boots and a pack. I told him I'd be up the following day.

As I drove up into the mountains I began to think about skiing again. It was nearly ten years since that autumn day when my brakes had failed completely going down a steep hill in the city. Rather than accelerate out of control, I had aimed the car for the nearest large tree and hit head-on. Several months later I was walking again but the doctor warned against skiing, telling me a bad fall could put me in a wheelchair for life. I had no intention of ever skiing again until Jorgy made visiting the basin sound so inviting.

Unfortunately, I had never really learned how to ski. So as I drove toward the mountains I began to worry about falling, and what might happen to my knees if I did. I hoped I was capable at least of skiing a mile and a half up a gently climbing road. When I reached Jorgy's ranch in the foothills, the news that distressed him I found reassuring. The storm just passed, which had closed the highway to cars for two days, had laid down four feet of powder that was going to slow us down. And another storm was on the way.

We left early the next morning in Jorgy's pickup, our skis and packs and two shovels in the back, his dog Missy between us in the well-heated cab. Snowline was quickly reached and we were stopped and instructed to put on chains. As we climbed toward Granite Basin the banks on either side of the road rose higher until the highway seemed a narrow, winding trench. Half a dozen snowplows were busily at work and the sparse traffic moved slowly under threatening skies. It began to snow hard and the radio warned that the highway might be closed at any moment. When we reached the Granite Basin road, blocked by three feet of fresh snow, the highway was closed for a distance of thirty-five miles.

We zipped up our parkas and got out in the heavily falling snow to shovel out a parking place, safe from passing snowplows, for the truck. Then, trailing our skis behind us, we set off up the road under towering twelve-foot snowbanks toward Granite Portals, a cabin where the completely unplowed portion of the road began. After half a mile's walk we should have reached the Portals, but nothing could be seen from the bottom of our trench.

Jorgy studied the treetops that rose above the snow, selected a spot and took off his pack to shovel a staircase up the vertical snowbank. When his series of steps led eight feet up the bank and he could reach no higher, he backed to the opposite side of the road and took a running jump at the improvised staircase. As

51

he struggled up I moved in beneath to give him a boost. His head was just above the rim when the stairway collapsed and we tumbled back down into the trench in a heap. With both of us shoveling it took another half-hour to build a new set of steps and clamber to the top of the bank.

Only then did we see Granite Portals, or rather the mound of snow that buried it. A tunnel led down to its second-story entrance. Even Jorgy was impressed: in fifteen winters he had never seen more snow. When we put on skis and packs and started toward the lake, we found it almost impossible to move. Where I had worried about falling on a slippery surface, our problem was one of forcing our way through sticky waist-deep snow. We plodded single file, our skis completely hidden beneath the uncompacted mass.

We moved slowly uphill through a handsome forest of big red fir. Their drooping blue-green needles were laden with snow and furrows in the dark red bark were plastered white. Moving as we were fifteen feet above the ground we couldn't see the faintest sign of the road, and with the smaller trees flattened or buried under drifts the country looked entirely unfamiliar. Jorgy knew where we were going, but it was slow, exhausting work. Each step meant lifting four feet of snow, and the sticky powder clung to the bottom of our skis. Every few yards we had to stop and help one another scrape off ten pounds of snow. We scarcely noticed that it was snowing hard and cold, and our clothes were soon damp with sweat.

Even though we took turns breaking trail every fifty yards or so, the leader was forced to stop for rest at least four times in that seemingly short distance. Jorgy admitted he had never seen harder going. All the cabins we passed were mere mounds in the snow, and we skied across a deeply buried power line that in summer was eighteen feet above the pavement.

When at last we reached the pass and came into the basin, we were met by a welcome breeze off the lake, and we stopped for a minute to cool off. Snow had stopped falling and there were patches of blue in the swirling clouds. It was my first look at Granite in midwinter, and the change was startling. Instead of a lake I saw a gently sloping valley of white. The drifts along the shores must have been thirty feet deep, and the vast slopes of

52

granite were now a smooth and featureless white.

Instead of running down the slope to Jorgy's cabin, we were forced to break trail all the way, then dig down to a second-floor porch that rose fifteen feet above the slope in summer. By the time we got inside it was almost four o'clock and the light outside was growing dim. The mile and a half trip from the highway had taken us nearly three hours. Our clothes were soaked with sweat and my legs were shaking with fatigue. While struggling to reach the cabin I had completely forgotten to worry about my knees, though both of us had fallen innumerable times and were thoroughly plastered with snow.

As Jorgy had expected, the power was off, but the phone was miraculously working. There was plenty of gas in the tank buried far beneath the snow, and the basement was well stocked with firewood. While I built a fire in the big stone fireplace, Jorgy lighted the gas heater and put on the coffee pot. Then he phoned to report the power failure. The man who answered found it hard to believe we had reached the basin. He said the highway had been closed for nearly four hours and supposedly no one remained on the summit. He hoped we had plenty to eat and drink because we might be snowed in for a week.

By the time Jorgy completed his call I was beginning to shiver in my thoroughly soaked clothes, despite having climbed halfway inside the fireplace. Jorgy produced a heap of clothes and we changed before the fire between gulps of scalding coffee as the room began to warm. Within an hour we were comfortable and dry. That night it cleared and turned intensely cold, and the next day was sunny and bright. Hoping to find a good crust on the lake, Jorgy set off up the basin on patrol, planning to return before the surface softened in the afternoon sun.

I was happy enough, once the day warmed up, to cautiously experiment on Jorgy's old skis on the slope below the cabin, where I could glide slowly downhill through the heavy snow. It was impossible to turn, and stopping meant taking a dive into the snow, but I gained a little confidence. On one run I ventured out onto the ice to inspect the black hole that marked the lake's outlet and returned across the roof of the buried Chalet.

Jorgy was back, somewhat discouraged, before midafternoon. The lake, he reported, wasn't settled enough for travel on skis. After repeatedly breaking through the thin, wind-formed crust, he had given up hope of patrolling both shores and had turned back well short of the channel. And since the few cabins he had passed were merely lumps in the snow, there wasn't very much he could learn of their condition. "And what could I have done if I'd found a caved-in roof? It was all I could do to keep my feet. The snow's got to settle before I can do a decent job."

We spent the rest of the short afternoon in the sun, leisurely shoveling the ten-foot layer of snow from Jorgy's nearly flat roof. "Right now," he said, "the load is pretty light, but let a warm rain hit a pack this deep and the weight would be enough to crush any cabin flat."

That night we were comfortable and warm before the fire in

54

our wood-walled cavern under the snow, and the following morning, again still and clear, we skied back out to the truck down the trench we had dug two days before. After two cold nights the pack was much firmer, and the traveling was easy, except when wet heavy snow fell off the trees onto our heads.

The highway was still closed, but the snowplows were working and we soon dug Jorgy's truck from its drift. Before noon we were driving down the empty road, drawing looks of surprise from the drivers of the snowplows we passed.

That was the first of the many winter trips I made with Jorgy to his cabin. Gradually I came to know his routine. Once we'd reached the cabin he would flip the nearest wall switch to check for electricity, then lift the receiver to check the phone. One or the other was nearly always dead. If the power was off he would anxiously open his freezer and sniff. His nose would tell him how long the line had been dead and how warm the weather in the basin had been.

I was more than a disinterested observer. Jorgy never saw the need to carry in fresh meat because frequent hunting trips kept his freezer well-stocked, but it meant we were dependent on the contents of that freezer for our dinner—whatever state they might be.

I have never known a man with a greater tolerance for over-ripe meat. In fact I'm not sure he doesn't prefer it. He would speak with enthusiasm of the richness of hamburger that must have weathered three or four power failures over a span of several winters. Only a strong stomach permitted me to swallow my share.

One cold night, after a hard trip in, Jorgy announced we were having a special treat for dinner. When we had finished off the tail end of a bottle of whiskey, he put enormous red steaks in the skillet to fry. They looked awfully good, if unusually lean, but their smell was definitely peculiar.

"This is bear," said Jorgy proudly, noticing me sniff, "and its flavor is quite a bit stronger than beef—in fact it's even stronger than venison. But if you like a good strong taste you're bound to like bear. It's a delicacy nowadays. Not many places there's enough of them to hunt."

When we were seated at the table in front of the fire, it took me just one bite to determine the source of that flavor.

"This meat isn't strong," I said, "it's spoiled!"

He took a large bite and chewed it thoughtfully. "It hasn't really turned yet. It's just a little gamy. You probably aren't used to strong meat. Especially bear." Then he proceeded to clean his plate and eat my steak, too, sopping up the last of the juice with bread. My only revenge was to eat three-quarters of the vegetables, soup and bread that completed our meal. That was the last time I depended on Jorgy's freezer for dinner. After that I made sure we carried in all the fresh meat we would need.

We spent a good many pleasant evenings in that cabin of Jorgy's, half of it buried deep in drifted snow, the other half looking out over the basin. On clear nights, with the lights turned off, starlight softly illumined the basin, and when the moon was full we could watch coyotes chase invisible snowshoe rabbits across the ice. During the day from our perch above the lake we could see clouds massing above the sugary wilderness summits beyond the basin, and by testing the wind it was easy to predict the progress of snow squalls headed down the basin. Every morning when the weather was mild, long gleaming icicles hung down in front of the windows like stalactites. Sometimes they grew to a length of four feet before afternoon sunshine or a breeze broke them off.

After a long day skiing through the basin we enjoyed an hour or two of gin rummy in the evening. We kept a running score of games won and lost that carried over from one year to the next. Jorgy usually won but one quiet evening, cut off from the world in a silent heavy snowfall that had closed the highway behind us, a remarkable thing happened: I could visualize every card in his hand. Every time he drew I knew what he had gotten. For perhaps half an hour on that still, snowy night, far from intrusions and distractions from without, I seemed to read his mind, and I won every game. After we quit I told him what had happened, but he preferred to attribute my success to luck.

When I first joined him on patrol, Jorgy had been at the lake fifteen years, and he had a lot of interesting tales to tell. I always like to hear about the early years, right after World War II, when outboard motors were small and unreliable. No one owned a boat that would plane, and cabin owners regularly rowed down the basin in skiffs. The Chalet maintained an old motordriven scow that chugged along the shores of both lakes every day, dropping off passengers, groceries, flamo, and mail, and picking up shopping lists and letters to be mailed. Life was quiet and slow.

In those days Jorgy and his family made their home in the basin. Late in the fall when the hunters were gone he cut firewood for a month and stocked up on flamo and food before snow closed the road. His two daughters skied out twice a day, no matter what the weather, to meet the school bus at the highway. To help meet expenses Jorgy casually ran the Chalet as a ski lodge for friends and customers willing to ski in.

The heart of his winter operation was a rope tow behind his cabin that ran three hundred feet to the ridge. A pulley at the top was fastened to a giant red fir and a shack at the bottom contained an ancient automobile engine. In-between, on the slope, pulleys were lashed to the limbs of strategically located trees. The engine was temperamental and the big manila rope often broke, but the lift usually ran through Easter week. Those were the years Jorgy seemed to like best. The work was hard and life often uncomfortable, but there was ample compensation in living on the edge of the wilderness.

In the days before my cabin was sufficiently hospitable for Jorgy's tastes, we customarily spent the night at his cabin, then set forth in the morning on skis, with small packs, up the southern shore of Lower Granite. There were times when the wind blew so hard in our faces that we could scarcely move against it. Though the sky was clear, blowing snow off the lake produced blizzard conditions that destroyed visibility and plastered us with white, while the sun was shining fifty feet above us. Half-blinded by the flying flakes we leaned into the wind, covering our numb faces with our arms, and when we stopped to rest we automatically turned, like horses in a storm, to put our backs to the wind. When the wind was strong we were glad for an excuse to get off the ice and into the shelter of the lakeside trees, and we often inspected protected cabins that didn't subscribe to Jorgy's service.

Other times on the lake, especially early in spring, the air might be so still that the hiss of our skis through the snow seemed loud, and when the sun was high above the white shining bowl it was often unbearably hot. Then sweat soaked our clothes and poured down into our boots, and more than once, to cool off, I stripped to my shorts on a mid-winter day and heaped my heavy clothing on top of my pack.

Between these two extremes were the common winter days when the basin was socked in, the peaks and ridges hidden, and the sun just a bright spot in the billowing cloud. The wind, though rarely fierce, seemed never to end, and snow squalls dogged us all day. Those were the days when numb faces and hands were a constant problem and our feet grew cold whenever we stopped. The only way to keep warm was to keep moving. When the weather was mean I would often leave Jorgy halfway up the lake. While he turned toward shore to look at a cabin I continued up the basin, skirting the open water at the mouth of the channel, and skied across the peninsula to my cabin.

After unlocking and forcing open the door, I pumped up the gasoline stove and lit it beneath a teakettle solid with ice. Then I lit the old kerosene heater, shoveled out the drift of snow that always lay inside the door, and laid out lunch. Half an hour later when Jorgy stomped the snow off his boots on the porch, the room was growing warm, the kettle was boiling, and the windows were clouded with steam. After a mug or two of boiling tea, he was sufficiently revived to dust the snow off his clothes and sit down for lunch.

If the weather was warm and still we would drag our chairs out onto the snow-free ledge and strip down to dry off in the sun, enjoying the view across Upper Granite. On those hot winter days we drank nearly frozen beer instead of hot tea. After lunch it was time to patrol the upper lake. Sometimes Jorgy would borrow a hammer and nails, or some plywood from the loft, to cover a broken window or nail shut a door forced open by the wind.

I generally stayed behind to clean up after lunch and make my own repairs. Then I would start up the lake after Jorgy, either following his tracks or heading straight across the lake to intercept him.

The upper lake, with its many coves and islands, is more interesting in winter than long and windy Lower Granite, and therefore more fun to patrol.

Once, when I overtook Jorgy near the head of the lake, he took me to see the pool of open water where Rainbow Creek spills into the lake. The snowbanks that ringed the pool had been packed hard by circling coyotes. In the bottom of the gravel-floored pool several dozen kokanee salmon were finning in the current. In that nearly freezing water they were sluggish and might easily have been caught by a coyote hungry enough to get wet. Whether any had gone fishing was impossible to tell. They may have been content to merely circle and watch, like the cat that stalks a bowl of goldfish.

On another trip, patrolling the upper lake after a tropical storm had dumped rain on soft snow, we looked up the north slope and noticed something odd about one of the highest cabins under Talking Mountain. Since the slope behind it was extremely steep and lay suspiciously close to several avalanche chutes, we sidestepped our way up the slope to have a look. A miniature avalanche had nudged the back of the cabin and tons of saturated snow still lay in a jumbled heap against the wall.

The blow had shoved the cabin from its foundations and would surely have sent it tumbling a hundred feet to the lake except for the presence of a tree growing close against the downhill wall. The little building was squeezed between the tree and the snowbank, its walls bulging but not actually broken. Aside from notifying the owner there was nothing to be done. In the summer the cabin was jacked back onto its foundations and the walls were straightened with an ingenious arrangement of levers and turnbuckles. Nearly ten years have passed and the cabin still stands, one of very few to survive an avalanche.

Another cabin, only a few hundred yards to the east, was not so lucky. Again we were patrolling after a freak warm rain had hit the basin in midwinter. As soon as we reached the upper lake we saw a trail of debris that ran down the cliff to the lake. The ledge on which the cabin had perched was bare. When we reached it we found the torrent of wet snow, or perhaps the powerful wind that it generated, had sheared off the cabin and thrown it down the cliff but left the floor entirely intact. It still serves as a platform for tents in the summer.

One spring, skiing alone up Lower Granite, I spotted half a cabin lying on its side on the lake. I looked up the slope and saw the other half twenty feet below its accustomed perch. Both halves were comparatively intact and, surprisingly enough, the stand of pine behind the cabin site was undamaged. Experts later concluded the avalanche that struck it was nearly spent, moving so slowly it filtered through the trees without knocking any down. But with the last of its momentum it tumbled the bulkier cabin from its foundations. The following summer the upper half was winched back up the slope and set back on its foundations, and most of the lumber from the lower half was salvaged.

Usually by the time we had patrolled Upper Granite, it was time to head down the basin, but if the weather was fair and there was plenty of daylight Jorgy was glad to return to my cabin for a quick mug of tea and a handful of oatmeal cookies from the sack we always carried. If shadows were approaching or the day was cold he refused to stop, afraid of the chill that damp clothes quickly bring. When it was time to go, Jorgy would cross the peninsula, then swing north to patrol along the head of Upper Granite while I stayed behind to close up the cabin. If my stay was brief I could ski across the peninsula and spot the two black dots, Jorgy and his dog, on their way across the ice to Mermaid Cove. Since I knew the route they'd take when they turned down the lake it was a simple matter to intercept them.

The first two years I traveled with Jorgy, we always returned to his comfortable cabin at the foot of Lower Granite for the night. Mine was too primitive and uncomfortable. But once the new Wedgewood, with its 20,000 BTU heater was installed, and the drafts were reduced by new windows and doors, I wanted to stay in my own cabin.

Jorgy was a little reluctant at first, but once the cabin was habitable we worked out a compromise. We spent the first night at his place and the second at mine, patrolling the upper lake in greater leisure and comfort. I spread a mattress on the floor in front of the stove for myself, while Jorgy slept with his dog Missy on the couch. I positioned my bed so that whenever I awoke— usually quite often—I could see the blue flame of the heater without moving. With the cabin half buried I didn't relish being asphyxiated if a draft blew out the low-burning flame. As small improvements gradually increased our comfort we enjoyed a good many nights in that cozy kitchen while wind-driven snow swirled against the windows.

One of our most memorable winter trips to the basin took place in the second week of May, when spring should already have begun. After a comparatively light snowfall early in the year, it stormed almost continuously through March and April. Jorgy hadn't been able to get into the basin for more than a month and he was anxious to see how the cabins had fared. Late-season wet snows were dangerous to cabin roofs and he feared there were some that might collapse if not shoveled—his own, for instance. So we headed for the basin as soon as the storm had blown itself out. As we skied up the road, laboriously breaking trail, Jorgy made notes of the roofs that must be shoveled before the next storm.

Jorgy's cabin, when we reached it, was in dangerous condition. There were ten feet of snow on the nearly flat roof, and the strain was clearly visible inside. One of the cracked rafters in the parlor had opened up, and only the winter brace directly beneath it had kept the roof from caving in. A beam in the kitchen was more critical still. Sagging beneath the tremendous weight of snow, it had driven its supporting post down into the floor, creating a two inch depression. Jorgy cautioned me not to walk near it, since the extra weight could bring down the roof. "She'll bounce back all right, once we get a little weight off, but don't let me forget to put a brace down below next summer. The floor wants a little more support."

The two-month storm had left other marks. There was no electricity, gas, or running water, and prolonged intense cold had frozen the spring and ruptured a pipe in the basement. "It must have been fairly cold," Jorgy observed. But his stoic acceptance turned quickly to rage when he lighted a lantern in the kitchen. Some animal—probably a weasel—had come down the chimney and gorged itself on the six dozen eggs that he had left in the kitchen back in March. Congealed frozen egg, embedded with crushed shell, was spread liberally throughout the kitchen.

It took more than an hour to clean up the worst of the mess, boiling water in a bucket propped on logs in the fireplace and using a mop to thaw the sticky coating. It was a great relief, when the kitchen was clean, to climb to the roof in the sun and fresh air to help Jorgy shovel the mountain of snow. It was a little like shoveling a sand dune at the beach, though we shoved great volumes off the edge of the roof the inroads we made were comparatively slight. And the heaviest snow, Jorgy explained, was on the bottom where the moisture was trapped.

The following morning was bright and clear and we shoveled for several hours before heading up the lake toward my cabin. Jorgy was making a careful inspection, circling each cabin before going to the next. Before we'd gone halfway a sudden wind came up, blowing snow in our faces, and clouds began to mass above the basin. Anxious to see how my cabin had survived, I left him and headed for the channel. Much of it flowed through a tunnel in the snow and the scarce open water where a snow bridge had fallen, was at least twelve feet below my skis. How could all that snow melt in less than two months? It looked like a snowbound summer for the basin.

By the time I reached the cabin the last of the blue was gone from the sky and it was snowing. The back of the cabin was buried under drifts but the loft door, as usual, was clear. Inside it was a clammy twenty-six degrees, but there was no sign of damage. The problem was turning on the gas. The flamo tanks stood against the outhouse wall, but there wasn't so much as a bump in the drift to suggest the location of that eight-foot-high building. I hunted for the shovel I had lashed to a tree six feet above the roof but there was no way to tell which treetop would lead down to it. Nothing looked familiar. I went back for a spare shovel and began to dig exploratory holes among the treetops.

On the third attempt I heard a muffled clang and dug down to release the missing shovel. Then I began the main excavation. By now it was steadily snowing, but windless. The snowpack was soft and my progress was good, but the deeper I went the wider I had to make my hole. There had to be room for me to stand and swing a shovel. After perhaps half an hour my shovel struck the outhouse roof six feet down. Relieved to find myself on target, I widened the hole until I could stand on the roof. When I dug the final foot and a half to the valves, there wasn't room to bend over to reach them. I had to climb halfway out of my well, then dive headfirst to the bottom. At last with numb fingers I opened the valve. I was happy to hear a "whoosh" in the line and see the pressure gauge jump to forty pounds.

Before I could move a voice asked "Having fun?" and Jorgy's grinning face appeared above me. He dragged me up by the ankles to the outhouse roof, then pulled me out of the hole. I hurried inside to light the stove, and though I didn't smell gas I couldn't be sure there wasn't a broken pipe beneath the snow. Time would tell. In the meantime we ate lunch and I dried my wet clothes. Gradually the kitchen began to warm. Snow was still falling when Jorgy, feeling restless, left to patrol a few upper lake cabins before dinner.

Two hours later, with the temperature up to sixty, I began to smell gas. When Jorgy returned he said it smelled to him like the bottom of the tank, not a leak. Was I sure the tank was full? I realized it wasn't, and the spare was empty. As though to offer confirmation the heater sputtered and went out.

Now we were definitely out of gas. Staying meant a cold dinner and a colder night, so we decided to retreat to the relative comfort of Jorgy's crippled cabin. Outside it was still snowing and visibility was low, but fortunately in May the days are long and light. Jorgy left immediately while I hurriedly packed up and locked the cabin. When I put on my skis I made a shocking discovery. The sole of my right ski boot had torn loose all the way back to the heel. It still locked securely into the binding, but any attempt to lift my right foot not only failed to lift the ski, it opened my boot like a gaping mouth and threatened to rip off the sole.

To take off the ski and unlock the cabin to try and make repairs would mean loosing contact with Jorgy. If I failed to appear he'd return to investigate, and by that time it would be dark and too dangerous to cross the lake. We'd be stuck for the night in a heatless cabin. Since snow conditions were good I decided to go ahead. Keeping my right ski flat on the snow and propelling myself with my left and my poles, I crossed the peninsula and started down the center of Lower Granite at top speed. Half a mile ahead, Jorgy and Missy were waiting, but the moment they saw I was on my way they turned and continued down the lake.

Not knowing how long my boot would hold together, I tried

hard to draw within shouting distance. If the sole ripped off and I was forced to walk I would break through the crust into thigh-deep snow. By the time I reached the middle of the lake it was snowing hard and the light was nearly gone. Both shores disappeared and I could barely make out the two black dots ahead. They, too, were hurrying to get home before dark, but by the time I reached the harbor I was close enough to yell and be heard.

To my relief Jorgy stopped to let me catch up, and he stayed by my side as I struggled up the slope to his cabin in the dark, dragging my right ski like a cripple. The power was back on and we celebrated our escape from a dismal night with rum in our coffee in front of the fire. The following morning, after shoveling another ton of snow off the roof, Jorgy lashed my boot together with baling wire, and I had no trouble, aside from wire-bruised toes, skiing out to the highway and the truck.

After several times being forced to dig down to turn on the gas in a snowstorm, I decided I needed better access to my flamo valves. The following fall, with the help of my friend Tim, I rigged a strange device that I hoped would make me independent of snow depth. We fastened a socket wrench into one end of a ten-foot aluminum pipe and set it snugly on the flamo valve. In the pipe's upper end a foot-long bar formed a handle. Theoretically, this crank, rising straight above the tank, would allow me to turn on the gas from fourteen feet above the ground.

The pipe was held erect by guy ropes tied to four trees and the socket was held in place by a wrapping of wire around the valve. To the handle we tied a red rag. Remembering that occasionally a valve froze shut I made sure before leaving that the valve was just barely closed.

On the first patrol trip with Jorgy that winter, I was shocked to discover that the flamo tank was empty. Wind in the trees that held the guy ropes had evidently turned the crank and opened the valve. In two months' time all my fuel had leaked away through the stove's four unlighted pilots.

The failure of the crank forced me to seek another solution. Jorgy suggested what should have been obvious: an inside shut-off that would allow me to leave the flamo valve open all winter. The following summer we put a valve in the gas main beneath the parlor floor, with a six-inch-square hatch for access. Several winters passed before I was sure the line had no leaks, but the system worked perfectly right from the start.

Unfortunately, the inside valve did not end my fuel problems. Twice within the next five winters I arrived in early spring to find the gas main broken between the inside valve and the stove. The unbelievable weight of settling snow had ripped the pipe from the metal strapping that held it to the floor joists and snapped it off at a connection. The first time, using a shovel on the snow and a hatchet on the ice, I laboriously tunneled my way to the break, shoved the pipes back together and wound the joint in a big ball of tape. Miraculously it lasted until summer. While replumbing the connection I doubled the strapping, but two winters later ice broke the pipe again.

This time the fireplace was roaring ten feet away when, smelling escaping gas, I lifted the hatch above the valve. Wind-driven gas gushed into the room and sent me reeling. Expecting the cabin to explode any moment, I slammed the hatch shut and tried to think what to do. Since the tanks outside were buried deep in drifts, the only place to stop the flow was at the inside valve. Holding my breath I jerked open the hatch, yanked the valve shut and slammed the hatch back in place. Then I threw open the doors and windows to let in fresh air and went outside to cool off. Though it was snowing hard, I was sweating.

The following summer, when I again replumbed the line, I added a ridiculous quantity of strapping and bracing, and though many trouble-free years have passed I am not at all sure my piping is safe. As I write, for example, the cabin sits in a pool of solid ice that reaches to the floor and my network of pipes is embedded like a fossil in a glacier. I'll be very much surprised if they survive the spring thaw intact.

Back in the days when I first stayed with Jorgy I used to shake my head at all the trouble he had with his power supply, thankful to be without electricity. But now that I look back on my struggle with butane, I see that his trials were inconsequential. At least he could phone for a repairman.

Those winter patrols with Jorgy ended ten years ago when he sold the Chalet and retired. But he kept the big cabin overlooking the lake, where we still often visit and play cards.

FIVE

Wildlife

A city-oriented friend once suggested that the cabin must be a sort of sanctuary from the wild creatures of the surrounding wilderness. That sounded reasonable enough, but when I thought about it later I realized just the opposite was true: the cabin was a gathering place *for* the region's wildlife.

Birds are always near the cabin and not a summer passes without a robin or an Oregon Junco flying in the door and beating its wings frantically against a window to get out, until Freda slips up from behind to gently capture it and take it outside. She has a way of speaking and moving that seems to soothe a trapped bird's fear. They may squawk and anxiously flutter at her approach, but they always allow themselves to be caught.

We are also accustomed to the thud of chicadees and juncos striking our windows from without, especially in early summer. One year in June, when snow still blanketed the ground, a flock of juncos bombarded our biggest kitchen window day after day. After each thump Freda would go outside and look for stunned or injured birds. Did they really want to get inside, we wondered, or were they merely feeding on the newly hatched swarms of insect life hovering beside the glass?

The cabin's most frequent visitors are golden mantle ground squirrels and chipmunks. Lured by the smells of food, they enter whenever opportunity allows. When the front and back doors, as well as the door between the rooms stand open, there is a corridor running the length of the cabin. Squirrels that come inside often get frightened and lose their sense of direction. We can't help laughing when an anxious squirrel, suddenly alarmed, spots distant daylight and scampers the full length of the cabin to safety, then looks around perplexed, wondering how the front porch turned into the back.

Sitting at the kitchen table we are accustomed to seeing a bold squirrel dash in the door, skid to a stop on the smooth pine floor and look around, sniffing the air. Then, following his nose, he turns into the pantry and mounts a shelf containing an open box of cereal or crackers. We hear a brief but wild scuffling, then he shoots from the pantry, cheeks bulging, slips as he makes the sharp turn through the door and disappears onto the porch. In less than a minute he has hidden his booty and is back for more.

Every summer there is a sizeable population of squirrels and chipmunks living under or close to the cabin—for good reason. Like other cabin owners, we put out all our food scraps for wildlife, but the real bonanza is Raff's big saucepan full of dogfood that sits on the porch by the kitchen door. No matter how much goes into it, that pan is cleaned and polished every day of the summer—and not by the old St. Bernard for whom it is intended!

Periodically, to check the demand for Rafferty's dinner, I put a heavy lid on the pan and we sit back to watch the fun. In less than five minutes the bluejays are raucously scolding from the porch rail while outraged squirrels jump up and down on the lid. It bangs and clatters, and occasionally an enterprising squirrel figures out how to lift one edge and crawl inside. When the lid clangs shut and he finds himself trapped, the racket is terrific until he manages to lift the heavy lid with his head and scramble out. Not a minute later, his entombment forgotten, he is once again trying to get in.

Once, when the clamor around the pan was particularly loud, I went out to take inventory. Two big squirrels were rocking the pan lid back and forth, while a bluejay and chipmunk looked on from the porch steps. A mother robin with three big speckled babies was patiently waiting in the path two yards away. Two more squirrels sat on an outcropping of rock near the pantry, and the gaudy red and yellow western tanager that regularly arrives between five and six o'clock for supper was perched at its

67

accustomed spot on the porch rail—although it was only mid-afternoon. Three or four bluejays squawked angrily, hopping from branch to branch, in the tree above the pan.

My appearance frightened none of this bold and hungry gang. It only served to raise the level of excitement. As I stepped to the pan there was a sudden great fluttering, scampering, squeaking, squawking, and beating of wings. I lifted off the lid, stepped back a few feet, and the rush was on: the bickering, complaining hungry horde descended. One would have thought they hadn't eaten in a week. It made me wonder how all this dogfood-eating wildlife gets through the winter without us.

When I visit the cabin in winter or spring, even though the ground is deeply covered with snow, if the weather is fair, I grow gradually aware of an increasing number of birds and squirrels. Though wilder than in summer, they seem to be waiting and watching for something, and they most often assemble near the kitchen door. I toss out my scraps and any food I can spare, and before I leave I always scatter several cups of dry kibble on the snow.

Bringing Raff's pan inside is almost as entertaining as putting on the lid—except when disoriented squirrels dash beneath the couch. Then we have to put the pan outside and leave the doors open until they are ready to come out—sometimes several days later. When the pan is inside, the permanent mouse population in the cabin celebrates with an all-night feast, but the mice at least, are quiet. While the pan is inaccessible, the creatures outside continuously and righteously complain. One night as we ate dinner a furious ground squirrel repeatedly jumped up to bang the bottom pane in the kitchen door, while bluejays perched in a tree near the window resentfully watched us eat.

Rafferty never takes the slightest notice of this activity, unless it keeps him awake. If he is sleeping on the porch, his nose beside the pan, it is not uncommon to see bluejays squawking in his ear and beating their wings above his head while ground squirrels run over his tail and dart beneath his nose. Finally the big dog takes the hint, gets wearily to his feet and moves off to find a quieter place to sleep.

There is no telling the numbers and kinds of wild things that

over the years have dined from Raff's pan, especially at night. Yellow bellied marmots have been seen gobbling kibble, so have our cone-cutting grey tree squirrels, the chickarees. One morning in late spring I found coyote tracks in the fresh snow leading to the pan. And I have no doubt that weasels and porcupines have paid it visits in the night. It wouldn't surprise me to walk out some day and see one of the grass-dwelling yellow striped garter snakes that live nearby in the grassy flat trying to swallow a lump of horsemeat. I have seen them beneath the porch, feeding on scraps that have fallen between the planks.

Quite often when we arrive to set up housekeeping for the summer we find a family of marmots living beneath the cabin or in one of the burrows in the rocks on the point. They remain perhaps a week before our presence drives them off, quietly departing in the night. Probably they can't get used to the shaggy St. Bernard who so closely resembles their natural enemy, the coyote. The fact that Rafferty sometimes sits on the roof of their burrow and barks, after thrusting his nose in its entrances to sniff, probably doesn't make them feel welcome.

One night during dinner we heard Raff on the back porch growling—something he rarely does. We hurried to the door to see him walking stiff-legged toward a bristling porcupine six feet away. Being cautious by nature he was moving very slowly, and he was only too happy to back away snarling when we called. With equal dignity the porcupine walked slowly down the steps, quills rustling softly, mounted the woodpile and leisurely climbed to the top of a pine. There he stopped and looked down. Raff sat alertly on the porch, looking up. An hour later when I passed, both were still looking and neither had moved. The porcupine was gone the following day, but Raff, when he remembered, continued to stare up that tree for a week.

Every few years a long-tailed weasel pays us a visit, brought no doubt by the abundance of rodents, squirrels, and birds, on which it preys. We suspect its presence when for no apparent reason the bluejays scream wildly and the chipmunks and ground squirrels, after squealing a warning, race madly for their holes. The pine marten's arrival is announced by the same sort of frenzy, but I have only seen this rare animal twice, once when it emerged from underneath the pier. The only other predator to inspire so much fear is the rare golden eagle that hunts in Granite Basin.

My favorite small animal—after the marmot—is the plump but feisty little cony. Conies are common in the basin whenever there are sheltering rock slides and ample supplies of nearby plant food. Also known as pikas or rock rabbits, these guinea-pig-like animals can be depended upon to stick their heads from their burrows and noisily scold intruders in their territory. Unfortunately none live within several hundred yards of the cabin.

Insects, of course, are hard to keep out of a cabin whose doors are often open all day in the summer, and around the roof and under the eaves there are gaps through which passage for the largest bugs is easy. So the cabin is home for a large permanent population of spiders, flies, moths, daddy longlegs, and so forth. Ants and mosquitos and ladybugs have their seasons. So do horseflies, deerflies, and bumblebees.

Granite Basin spiders, though harmless to most humans (they sometimes bite me), are the most persistent web builders I have ever encountered. We keep an old-fashioned feather duster with a long handle by the fireplace to periodically clean out the corners, but within forty-eight hours of a fairly thorough dusting there are extensive new webs throughout the cabin. And, if we should leave the cabin for a week, we return to find incredible wall-to-wall webs that wrap themselves around our heads as we walk. Perhaps the shortness of the summer has something to do with the prodigious spinning of our spiders.

Despite the spider population, flies abound in the cabin. The combination of shelter and food must hold a strong attraction, and of course it isn't hard to get in. In midsummer their ability to multiply is unpleasantly amazing. I returned one July from a week in the backcountry to find literally hundreds of flies at each kitchen window. There was a drone in the room like a hive full of bees. It took me more than an hour of swatting to dispatch them. After cleaning up the bodies I went outside for fresh air and spent an hour canoeing on the lake.

But when I returned another hundred flies were crawling on the windows, and I reluctantly went back to work. The following morning I awoke to the sound of humming downstairs. To my surprise and disgust I found the kitchen alive again with flies. Where could they be coming from, and why? A little thought led me to the open garbage pail beneath the sink. It was black with flies. And when I took it outside for closer inspection I found its walls covered with bulging white eggs. Half a dozen hatched into flies as I watched. Once the breeding ground was gone (I dumped the eggs in the lake to feed the trout), the problem was solved.

Small pale moths may be seen every evening fluttering around the cabin while their larger relatives make suicidal swoops at the candles, gas lights, and gasoline lanterns. Compared to flies and spiders they make very little trouble and we think of them as friends. The daddy longlegs that creep around at night on their two-inch legs are not so welcome, especially to Freda. We customarily spend the summer evenings after dark reading in the kitchen. Freda's spot is the sagging couch, which evidently is home to dozens of families of daddy longlegs. After spending the day in the dark among the springs, they like to go walking in the evening.

Half an hour after she gets settled Freda will spot the advance guard walking slowly up her pantleg. Unwilling to kill anything, she flicks it to the floor with a sigh and goes on reading. Twenty minutes later it is back—along with its cousins. She shoos them angrily away, noticing in the process that half a dozen others are advancing up the couch. When a large specimen steps daintily from her hand onto the page of her book she jumps up to shake it off and sweep the couch clear of crawling insects. On nights when the daddy longlegs are especially restless, she may get up several times to brush them from her clothes. Much as they annoy her she won't let me fumigate the couch.

The successive waves of insects that visit the cabin appear in dependable progression each year. When we first arrive and snow still covers the ground there are only sluggish houseflies and semi-torpid spiders. The first seasonal arrivals are the ladybugs. Some years they come by the millions. For a week or more they are everywhere outside. They sit like rows of red beads on our windowsills, and gradually work their way inside, turning up in our food, on our clothes, and even in our beds. Other years we see only a handful. The number that reach the basin depend on the wind. Every spring ladybugs breed in the lowlands to the west. Part of the ceremony involves flying in swarms several thousand feet above the ground. If the prevailing west wind is blowing strongly, millions of bugs are carried up into the mountains. Perhaps the unexpected journey annoys them, for the ladybugs at Granite occasionally bite.

By the time the snow has been gone a week and the weather has turned warm, the first mosquitos of summer appear. About the same time flies begin to breed, and the spiders spin their webs day and night. Within a week of the first mosquito bite, the season is at its height. For the next several weeks we keep the doors closed and open only windows that have screens. If the summer is dry, as it usually is, mosquitos are scarce by the end of July, except out on the lake in the evening.

The mosquitos of July are succeeded by the big biting horseflies of August, and toward the end of the month they are joined by their wicked little cousins, the deerflies. Fortunately, on our side of the lake, their numbers are small and they are slow enough to be easy to swat before they bite. By August the half-inch-long black ants have found their way into the cabin. If a light is held close to the kitchen floor at night they can be found in fair numbers methodically scavenging for crumbs. With the onset of autumn, unless the summer has been wet, the cabin's insect life is considerably reduced. Only flies and spiders remain in any numbers.

Every year in late June, about the time the first mosquitos appear, we watch for the miraculous emergence of the dragon-fly. When the first crawling nymphs have been sighted we stretch out on the old mattress on the pier to observe the metamorphosis. All around the harbor on pier supports, boat hulls, trees, rocks, and grass stems, two-inch-long nymphs the color of mud climb slowly from the lake where they have lived for a year on the bottom of the cove.

The stifflegged crawl ends no more than a foot above the water. Here the weary nymph stops, digs in his claws and turns as still as death. After anywhere from thirty minutes to two hours a split develops down the length of the back, the head falls forward as though hinged, and a soggy creature of indeterminate shape begins to struggle through the opening. Once it climbs free of the now translucent skin, its wet, accordioned body begins to lengthen. Within minutes it is twice as long as the shell, and glistening lacy wings of even greater length unfold. Within an hour the damp colorless creature has been trans-formed into a brilliant blue dragonfly. As though freshly coated with fast-drying lacquer, its wings and body grow shiny and taut. It sits motionless, drying, a few minutes longer, then all at once its wings begin to quiver. A moment later it is effortlessly, grace-fully flying above the cove—only two or three hours from the time it walked the bottom of the lake.

For the next several days dragonflies are everywhere—hatch-ing, drying and flying. In the air as underwater these big insects are predators, and their favorite food is the equally newborn mosquito. Only hours after hatching the dragonfly is ready to mate, and we see swooping pairs flying tandem above the water, the thorax of the female stuck securely to the tail of the male.

Fertilized eggs are dropped in the shallows or tucked in stems of water grass, where they hatch into nymphs that will live on the floor of the cove until next June.

Though we have yet to find one inside the cabin, western fence lizards live on the sunny bluff behind the cove, where their charcoal brown bodies blend nicely with camouflaging lichens. They stand out only when courting males do their restless rhythmic pushups or inflate their iridescent blue throats.

Eating lunch on a rock one April day, I became aware of a courting pair nearby. The nearly black male with the bright blue belly was aggressively pursuing a smaller brown white-bellied female. After a series of courting pushups failed to impress her, he sprang onto her back. When she shrugged him off and began to move away he rushed in from the flank to clamp his jaws on her shoulder and hang on.

She struggled on a few steps, dragging her admirer, then apparently vexed she turned to bite him on the base of one hind leg. He reluctantly let go to shake his bleeding leg, then attempted again to climb on her back. Since she made no attempt to escape these advances, I had to conclude she enjoyed them. For half an hour the brutal ritual continued, neither participant showing the slightest interest in my presence, although I was only three feet away.

Poisonous snakes don't come to Granite Lakes, though twenty miles away they are common. The absence of abundant feed and the long, heavy winters offer migrating rattlesnakes little incentive to climb the steep creek that leads into the basin. But Freda didn't know that. To her any snake might be poisonous. Alone in the cabin one August afternoon she opened the cooler and bent down for potatoes. Coiled beside the bag was a strange brown snake about two feet long. She jumped backward, slammed the door, and sat down to think.

I was away and not due to return for several days. She couldn't get along without her cooler that long, but she wasn't prepared to open that door. She put on a jacket and walked up the shore to the next inhabited cabin. There she found our friend Walter, who agreed to have a look at the snake. Back in our kitchen he gently opened the cooler and closed it. The snake hadn't moved. He didn't recognize it as a Rubber Boa, a harmless relative of the boa constrictor, but he knew it wasn't a rattler.

When next he opened the door, he was ready with a large plastic jar and a spatula. The comparatively sluggish boa allowed itself to be coaxed inside, after which, at Freda's request, it was released in a patch of brush a considerable distance from the cabin. We never were able to determine how that snake got into the cooler, a feat never managed by the cabin's mice, which, probably, it was hunting.

Several years later, on my way to the outhouse, I nearly stepped on another coiled boa in the middle of the path. Since it appeared to be sleeping, I called Freda and Kath and we took a close look before I gently moved it to the shelter of a nearby thicket. It was hard to believe that this oversized brown worm could subsist by catching mice, squirrels, and other reptiles, and killing them by squeezing in the coils of its strong constrictor body.

When we move in for the summer, usually sometime in June, the stream beneath the cabin is always flowing strongly, its waters spreading out in the grassy flat behind the cove. This is the time of year when the misnamed Pacific Treefrog (which has no interest in trees) is spawning in running water and ponds. The males inflate their throat pouches once the sun goes down and produce a loud mating call—*krek-ek, krek-ek*—at one-second intervals.

For a week or two, mating frogs in the grass, underneath the cabin, and in the nearby snow pool keep up a steady din. There must be hundreds in the chorus and the pulsating roar can be deafening. After the quiet nights of early spring, it's hard to sleep those first few evenings that the treefrogs sing.

Once accustomed to the sound I almost cease to hear it, but I am liable to wake if it suddenly changes or stops. Then, scarcely two weeks from the time it began, the nightly chorus begins to fade. I may wake a week later to incredible stillness, a perfect absence of sound, and wonder when it was that the treefrogs stopped croaking.

One utterly still evening in early October I was alone in the cabin, reading before the fire, when from under the floor very near where I sat came the *krek-ek, krek-ek* of a solitary treefrog.

75

I took a flashlight to the hatch in the floor and looked around. There he sat in the long-dry streambed, a lonely little frog crying for his mate. I slipped the hatch back in place and the calling resumed for several minutes before it stopped for good. The night seemed very still without it.

The following morning, my first at the cabin after three weeks away, I was sitting in the sun on the porch eating breakfast when I realized the usual wildlife was missing. There wasn't a squirrel or chipmunk to be seen, not a bluejay or robin or chickaree. I wondered where they'd gone and how they were faring without the food we had provided all summer. Could we have made them too dependent? What if we'd deprived them of the ability to hunt or the urge to store food for the winter? Then I saw a pair of eyes looking out from a heap of granite left over from building the chimney. I tossed a scrap of bread and out came a ground squirrel to get it.

Before he disappeared into his fortress, a chipmunk came down a tree and looked around expectantly. I tossed a crumb on the porch and he came to get it. A bluejay appeared and the first squirrel returned. I went in the house for more bread. In less than ten minutes there were a total of four ground squirrels, two bluejays, two chipmunks, and a robin all squawking and chattering and racing one another for bread scraps. It was just like summer. All the creatures I'd imagined wandering hungry in the wilds had taken up permanent residence near the cabin.

The bright and bouncy chickaree that nests in a tree on the edge of the swamp is always close by. We are often awakened early in the morning by the fall of pine cones on the porch. He follows them down, settles himself on his haunches on the rail and proceeds to attack them like a hungry man eating corn on the cob. One by one he bites off the scales, shucks the seed from its husk and pops it in his mouth. When he is done there is nothing but a small ragged core and a neat heap of scales.

The chickaree's call is a prolonged fading whinny that makes one think of a horse. On still days in the fall we often hear it clear across the lake. If its call is imitated the chickaree will invariably stop and look around until it sees it is only a human, then it flicks its tail several times in annoyance and hurries on its way.

Occasional loud thumps on the roof late at night, followed by the scampering of feet, make me suspect we are visited now and then by the nocturnal and rarely seen northern flying squirrel, which forages while other squirrels sleep. A neighbor up the lake, after similar thumps, stayed up several evenings and finally got a glimpse of a small big-eyed squirrel with furry webs between its front and hind legs. When it stretches its legs the web becomes a wing that enables the little rodent to glide safely through the air from the top of a tree, landing as much as a hundred feet away.

There is considerable bird life close to the cabin, though I can only identify the commoner species. One of my favorites is a California gull that often perches on the peak of the roof. Perhaps from that height he can spot the small surface-feeding trout on which he lives.

Every spring a pair of robins is sure to nest in one of the pines near the cabin. Sometimes they build, sometimes they move into an existing nest, perhaps one they built the previous year. Once the eggs have been laid we often notice the changing of the guard, when the foraging bird relieves its mate on the nest.

For several weeks the adults take turns sitting on the eggs, then one day we look up and the nest seems empty. Inspecting the ground at the foot of the tree we usually find pieces of blue eggshell. Now the really frantic foraging begins. From our bed at dawn we hear the quiet purling conversation of the parents as they plan a day which will be wholly devoted to feeding their voracious young. Every few minutes throughout the hours of daylight a parent lands with a beakful of food.

In less than a week each arrival at the nest sets off a clamorous chorus, and we look up to see four or five eagerly upraised, wide-open beaks noisily begging to be fed. From the first light of dawn until well after dark the energetic parents can be seen flying back and forth across the lake to the lush vegetation at the back of Cornell Cove where the hunting for worms and insects must be good.

Then one morning we're aware that it's strangely quiet, and we look up to see the nest is empty again. For the following week we have to be careful where we put our feet. We have often nearly tramped a well-camouflaged baby robin sitting motionless, as instructed, in the middle of a path. The easiest way to locate the young is by spotting the anxiously coaching parents as they hop about nervously, offering a steady stream of advice. The fat but clumsy babies are highly vulnerable now as they learn how to forage and fly, and we often find one who didn't survive those first few demanding days beyond the nest.

The survival rate of baby robins near the cabin is certainly aided by the presence of Rafferty's well-stocked pan. An important part of foraging, it seems, is learning to eat dogfood on the porch. As soon as the babies, whose fluffy coats make them look larger than their parents, can be assembled in the path at the end of the porch, the lesson begins. The mother robin demonstrates for her three or four wondering chicks. After looking about for enemies, she hops to the pan, chases out a squirrel, selects a moist kibble and hops back to present it to her babies.

When they have eagerly gobbled it she hops back toward the pan, urging them to follow. They hop a few steps and stop, uncertain. She continues to the pan and patiently collects another kibble. As the process is repeated she gradually works them closer, until they finally understand and dip their beaks in the pan while she stands guard. Once they can find the pan and feed without help, they are on their own.

Among the creatures near the cabin, there is a pecking order of sorts, and it isn't based entirely on boldness. The bloodthirsty little weasel receives the most respect, but the businesslike robin comes second. When it is nesting or raising young it is absolutely fearless and will attack any creature that threatens. Next come the golden mantle ground squirrels which easily intimidate the bigger Steller jays. The noisy but nervous nutcracker follows, trailed by careful chipmunks, unassertive juncos, cautious chickarees, and timid tanagers.

There are larger animals that live in the basin but they tend to keep their distance from people. There isn't enough cover or feed near our cabin to bring the mule deer to graze, but they are common across the channel where the hemlock forests are thick, and they can generally be found on the basin's high ridges. Neighbors up the lake put out salt in the well-wooded draw behind their cabin for the deer who come to visit in the evening.

The coyote population tends to fluctuate according to the supply of snowshoe rabbits, its favorite dinner. Both are secretive: the rabbit is shy, the coyote sly. Few of either are seen in the basin but their populations are probably substantial. At least there is no shortage of tracks. Coyotes are frequently seen in midwinter when their calls fill the basin almost nightly. In spring and fall their varied songs are common, and now and then we hear one close by in midsummer.

An upper lake friend, while we were walking in a high remote backcountry valley, showed me the partial remains of a deer. A few years before he'd stumbled upon the still bleeding carcass. He was wondering what had killed it when he heard a low growl and looked up into the eyes of an approaching mountain lion. It was then, he said, that his collegiate experience on the track team served him well. He was sure he had never run faster.

The cabin's real owners, dating back probably to the year it was built, are the white-footed deer mice that live in the walls. When we first moved in we vaguely knew there were mice. There were nests in the woodpile, droppings in the pantry, chewed knotholes, shredded clothing, well-used mousetraps, and other strong evidence—like gnawing sounds in the walls at night and scurrying footsteps in the dusty loft.

Every night that first summer when I lay down to read, a mouse was chewing in the wall behind my head. I would slap the wall with the palm of my hand, making Freda jump. After a minute of silence the gnawing would resume. Within a night or two my slaps had lost all effect. The same thing happened one night in the wall at the head of our bed. Smacking the wall stopped the noise almost long enough to get to sleep—but not quite. Finally I got up and went outside to sleep on the mattress on the pier.

Our policy toward mice is somewhat inconsistent. Like everyone else we spread poisoned grain in the fall to protect our food and bedding, but any mice we actually see come under our protection.

The discovery of nesting mice is a common early-summer occurrence. Freda found a mother and nesting babies settled comfortably in her sewing basket. I reached into a bag for steel wool one day and grabbed a wriggling mouse instead. Freda carefully pulled out a drawer in the desk to show me a mother and five babies lying luxuriously on a bed of cotton from the first aid kit. She gently closed the drawer and the next time we looked, a week or two later, they were gone.

One morning Kath was wakened in her bed beneath the eaves by the sound of light scuffling. On the floor a yard away a mother mouse was squeaking instructions to three babies. The corner of her blanket was lying on the floor and the four mice ran up it and onto the bed. When Kath reached out to pet them they hastily scurried away.

In the first few years we were much too busy to give our mouse population much thought. The cabin was a sieve: they could come and go as they liked. I'm sure we believed we'd get rid of them in time. Until then we'd simply have to hang our clothes in plastic bags, keep the plate rail free of breakables and store food in metal containers. Our mattresses we wrapped in canvas and left on the beds, hoping for the best but often in the spring we found them drilled with one-inch diameter tunnels. There was only one mouseproof chamber in the cabin: the stout kitchen woodbox. We emptied and cleaned it and Freda used it for food, but we never could be sure mice wouldn't chew their way in.

It wasn't until we began to remodel that we realized the extent to which our mice were entrenched. When we removed a portion of the paneling in the parlor we were amazed to find that the four-inch-deep space between inner and outer walls was one continuous mouse nest, standing four to six feet high! Its principal ingredients were kapok, feathers and greenish wool. There was no telling how many mattresses, pillows and army blankets over the years had been shredded and bit by bit carried inside the walls.

At first we thoughtlessly scooped out the nest, filling box after box, and took it outside to burn. But the futility of removal soon became apparent. If we took their nest away the mice would simply replace it—at our expense. They were too well dug in to ever be driven out. The cabin would have to be entirely dismantled and lined with tin to keep mice from living in the walls.

So we told ourselves the nest made excellent if unconventional insulation, and we left it in place when we remodeled. The discovery that we lived inside a wrap-around mouse nest was disconcerting at first, but soon we came to accept and even forget it. We were simply guests who brought gifts of food and nesting material to pay for our temporary use of the cabin.

One evening after dinner when I came in from fishing, Freda complained that some creature was caught in the back of the pantry behind the gas fridge. She thought it was a bird. The crying and scratching could be heard throughout the cabin, but when I looked with a flashlight there was nothing to be seen. We went outside and put our ears to the wall until we found the source of the noise. Then, laughing and swearing, while Freda held the flashlight, I pried away the siding. The moment it came loose a tiny deer mouse shot out and disappeared under the cabin.

The dog biscuit mystery also taught us something new. One morning I came downstairs from the loft to find one of Rafferty's dog biscuits lying on the landing. I picked it up and returned it to the box in the pantry. The next morning another biscuit was waiting in its place. The third morning, finding yet another biscuit, I got down on my hands and knees to look around. Where three boards met at the foot of the stairs there was a gap a little larger than a keyhole. I wouldn't have believed a mouse could pass through, but there was mouse fur caught in the gnawed, splintered wood. Three nights in a row the mouse who lived inside had dragged a dog biscuit half the length of the cabin and hoisted it up two steps to the landing. But there he'd been forced to leave it behind for it was three times the size of his hole.

Mice, like other creatures, are subject to population cycles. We arrived one spring at the height of the cycle. The mouse population had exploded. Instead of one mouse occasionally gnawing in the walls, there were always two or three. Every night after dark there was scuffling in the pantry as they moved from box to box. We saw them scampering in the shadows, heard them rustling in the garbage and empty tin cans. We found a groggy mouse happily licking out an empty wine bottle while his brother cleaned a cider jug. When we talked to our neighbors we found it was the same in every cabin. The basin was teeming with mice.

We thought of putting out poison to thin the herd, but with the crumbs on the floor and Raff's pan on the porch we knew it would only be ignored. Besides, our neighbors had already tried it without success. One of them in desperation set out eight traps before going to bed. Throughout the night the household was awakened periodically by loud snaps. In the morning there were mice in all eight traps, but no one had slept very well and no one wanted to empty and rebait the traps.

Their next door neighbors devised a quieter procedure for dealing with the horde. They put a lump of smelly cheese in the bottom of a cardboard carton and leaned a stick against it to serve as a runway. As soon as they went to bed they began to hear the faint thump of mice falling into the box. The lump of cheese was gone by morning and they had captured twenty mice, which were set free in the woods a quarter-mile away. Inside of a week there were as many mice as before.

Every cabin that summer had similar experiences. A friend found a newborn mouse huddling in a corner and, taking pity, put it in a box along with water and food. The next morning three more babies had somehow moved in.

A lower laker, who had never before had mice, put out five pounds of poisoned grain the week before her guests were due from the city. When a visiting ladyfriend exclaimed, "I could swear I saw a mouse run out of the kitchen!" the hostess replied, "Don't pay any attention, it only encourages them."

The culmination of the invasion, as far as I was concerned, came late one August evening. Reading on the couch by lantern light I saw a mouse shoot out of the pantry and head for the garbage pail under the sink. In a shaft of moonlight coming in the window, a second mouse was prospecting the counter for crumbs. I put down my book and turned off the lantern. By the time my eyes had adjusted to the moonlight there were three mice at work on the counter and two more were licking the grease off the stove.

A pair began fighting in the middle of the floor and two more ran squeaking from the pantry. In the wall beside me, on the plate rail above me, and in the loft where Kath and Freda were sleeping, I could hear the faint drumming of tiny running feet. Glass clinked on a shelf, paper ripped in the pantry, the sound of gnawing came from under the sink. I jumped as a grey form ran across my legs. The cabin was literally alive with mice. After watching awhile I went upstairs to bed, but before climbing in I took a close look between the sheets. More than one neighbor had found a mouse in his bed.

A week or two later the summer was over. We dumped the last of the garbage, gave the kitchen floor a scrubbing to get rid of stray scraps, and took pains to store our food in dependably mouseproof containers. Then we spread three times the usual quantity of poisoned grain and closed the cabin, hoping that somehow the bumper mouse crop would disappear. And it did. Whether it was the long cold winter that followed, a change in the breeding cycle, or a scarcity of food we never found out. But the following summer, things were back to normal—we heard only one mouse at a time in the walls.

SIX

Trout

Trout and wilderness mountains have always been closely linked in my mind. Where trout can flourish, I've always thought, so can I. My fondness for trout, to a large extent, reflects my fondness for the country in which they live—the sort of country Granite Basin typifies.

When I was young I wanted to fish all day and half the night. Each strike was a thrill, and the quivering tug of a fighting trout seemed the very essence of pleasure. To capture trout with flies I tied myself was more satisfying still. I simply couldn't get enough. Although I never wasted fish, even if it was hard to find people who would eat them, it never occurred to me to let any go. In those early years I was a legal but somewhat greedy angler.

By the time we bought the cabin I had probably caught a thousand trout, and my fervor had begun to diminish. But owning a cabin on the edge of a trout lake made fishing irresistibly convenient, and Freda liked fresh-caught trout served with lemon. So we kept a sack containing a mixture of cornmeal, cornstarch, salt, pepper, and half a dozen spices. I would walk in the door with a freshly caught rainbow of eight or nine inches, clean it in the sink, shake the damp fish in the spice mix and give it to Freda to cook along with dinner.

In the early days, when the work of rebuilding the cabin seemed unending, an hour's flycasting in the evening provided marvelous relaxation. I soon learned that the granite bluff between our cove and the channel offered fishing as good as any on Upper Granite. The water was deep, the prevailing wind produced a current along the rock, and the bluff afforded both casting room and a helpful view of cruising fish. So most of the time a fishing excursion took me less than a hundred yards from my door.

I kept my three-ounce glass fly rod set up and ready in a sheltered nook in the rock behind the tree that grows up through the pier. A number twelve mosquito, at the end of a 7½-foot tapered leader, was hooked near the reel seat. Since the rod stood waiting fifty feet from the kitchen and was ready to use in a matter of seconds, I could profitably go fishing ten minutes before dinner would be served.

Over the years, as I came to know the lake and grew accustomed to taking trout, I no longer needed to kill everything I hooked. At first I released only undersized fish, but with the passage of the years I found increasing satisfaction in putting back all fish I didn't need, regardless of size. Young trout, I decided, deserved some protection from foolish impulses—like striking at artificial flies.

Fishing with flies, unlike hardware or bait, usually does little damage since the fish is hooked in the mouth, not the throat. After playing a trout until it's too tired to thrash, I reach underwater with my left hand and grasp it gently but firmly just behind the gills. With my right hand I grab the protruding fly at its base. Moving it gently, I discover how it's hooked, then with a circular movement I take the pressure off the barb and back it out. Usually this operation can be completed underwater in a matter of seconds, and the trout darts away without permanent damage.

My first trips to the wilderness beyond Granite Basin were mainly to fish in the dozens of small lakes in glacial cirques. But gradually my interest turned to the country itself, and now I often find myself on remote, seldom-fished trout water without a rod—although sometimes I curse my improvidence. In the spring, after months away from trout, the urge to fish is often strong, so with friends I make a trip to back-country lakes where the fly fishing is dependably good. If we're lucky we catch all we can eat, plus a few more to bring home for our families. After that I only fish casually the rest of the summer—unless we get hungry for trout.

Though my eagerness to fish has gradually declined, my enthusiasm for the noble trout has not diminished in the least. Where once I had to catch them, I now find great pleasure in observing them and discovering their habits. When conditions are right I can sit for hours and watch the Granite trout as they cruise and feed, compete and court, without a thought of trying to catch them. In fact the more I watch, the less I want to fish. Trout I've observed I tend to think of as friends.

One still July morning I was sitting in a natural rock seat at the foot of the bluff, gazing down through the still, clear water of Upper Granite. Small waves washed over my bare feet and slapped against the rock, making a popping sound as they filled a tiny cave. Below the surface the bluff dropped three or four feet to a sloping pebbled bottom that reflected the ripples on the gently moving surface. Two small rainbows cruised confidently into my field of vision, moving unhurriedly until one or the other would spot a promising particle. Then, propelling itself with its tail, it would engulf the floating morsel, quickly spitting out those that proved to be inedible. Their pink sides and youthful parr marks were visible whenever they turned.

A ladybug landed upside down on the water and struggled desperately to turn upright and escape. The commotion stirred the water and was reflected on the bottom, but it was nearly a minute before the thrashing bug entered the narrow field of view of one of the trout. Racing upward, mouth open, the little fish broke the surface but missed the bug by an inch. It darted this way and that in excited confusion, until finally it happened on the bug and sucked it in. After repeated convulsive swallowing it returned to the level at which it had been cruising.

A loud splash about thirty feet offshore turned my attention to the widening concentric rings that marked the rise of a heavy fish and, by the time I turned back to the scene at my feet, a dignified brook trout, twice the size of the young rainbows had appeared from the direction of the cove. Unlike the little fish he cruised slowly and sedately, moving parallel to the bluff and only a foot below the surface. The milk-white borders of his barely moving fins identified both his maturity and breed. He appeared to take no notice of the frolicking rainbows though he passed within a yard of where they played with their food.

86

Moving deliberately, the old brook disappeared in the direction
of the channel.

When he was gone my attention returned to the rainbows,
but a movement in the depths at the edge of visibility caught my
eye. I slowly raised my hands to form slits before my eyes
(making "Indian sunglasses" the old timers call it) and searched
the green haze for a form. A large motionless trout, probably a
rainbow, took shape in the depths and drifted slowly inshore. I
sat perfectly still, but something made him change his mind—
perhaps the midday light in the shallows was too bright—for he
leisurely turned and sank back into the depths. The little rainbows played on as though nothing had happened, and I guessed
they had not seen a fish large enough to eat them both for
breakfast.

From out of the channel came two boys in a small pram, one
rowing, the other holding a pair of spinning rods. They tied the
boat to a rock about fifty feet away, climbed the bluff and,

standing side by side, began hurling spinners into the lake and reeling them in. Almost at once two good-sized rainbows, obviously startled, hurried past me from the direction of the fishermen. They were followed soon after by three smaller and less agitated fish, which in turn were trailed by the unruffled, dignified old brook trout. Then a sudden breeze ruffled the surface, drawing a curtain across my window in the water.

The biggest trout I've seen in Upper Granite lay among the pilings beneath the pier. I discovered him accidentally long after dark. I'd been out canoeing and was using my flashlight to moor the boat securely, when the beam of light cast a shadow on the bottom. Though I turned the beam straight on him, the fish never moved. For perhaps five minutes I watched the big trout, his fins scarcely moving; then a gust blurred the surface. When it cleared a moment later he was gone.

In the evening after dinner, when boat traffic has ceased for the day and trout are likely to be rising, I love to go canoeing on the lake with my flyrod. My first stop is the reef, a barely submerged peninsula of rock only seventy yards from the pier. If good fish are rising I coast to within twenty feet, then, balanced on my knees, cast upwind to all the sheltered nooks I have discovered while swimming underwater. When all the promising lies have been covered, I paddle to another rock favored by trout, this one between the channel and the mouth of Cornell Cove.

Once I'm out in the canoe, if the evening is pleasant, I may explore the other places that in the past have yielded fish. After a swing through Cornell Cove, which is pretty but usually unproductive, I direct a few casts beneath the overhanging alder in deep water just beyond it, where good trout often shelter and feed on the insects that drop from the thicket.

Next down the shore is the shallow sandy flat where a small stream emerges from the foot of an avalanche chute. The setting is lovely and seems to promise feeding trout, but so far it hasn't produced a good fish. Another area I visit because it intrigues me is the broad, shallow channel between Picnic Island and a willow-grown avalanche chute on the mainland. Even though I know the general configuration of the bottom, I always hit rocks and run aground after dusk, but there are several deep holes that appeal for some reason to the brook trout that descend from Rainbow Lake above.

By the time I've gone this far I'm usually tired of fishing (whether I've caught anything doesn't really matter) and I stow my rod in the bottom of the boat and paddle on to the top of the lake. If I happen to find a good fish feeding eagerly I can always pick up the rod for a cast or two. Or if trout are rising well when I turn for home, I may strip off fifty feet of line and let it stretch out behind the slow-moving canoe, trolling a fly on the surface.

At the head of the lake I like to paddle up a hidden channel to the foot of a waterfall. Holding onto a tree limb in the foaming pool I enjoy the crash of falling water, the tug of the current in the darkness and the smell of rank vegetation. Then, pulled by the current, I drift down the creek and back into the quiet of the lake.

If the evening is fine I'm sure to meet friends in kayaks, canoes, or rowboats, who are fishing or cruising through the balmy dusk. Happy to stop and visit under such pleasant circumstances, we catch one another's gunwales and talk for a while as we slowly drift in the gathering darkness. It's not at all unusual to see three or four boats drifting together at dusk among the islands. And, quite often, as the night grows cooler, we adjourn to someone's cabin for tea, wine, or beer and more conversation by candlelight. Freda never worries if I go fishing "for an hour" after dinner and fail to return before midnight.

***

Granite Basin was dug from the monolithic granite some two million years ago by a succession of glaciers flowing east. Melting ice gradually filled the resulting depression to form Upper and Lower Granite Lakes. For a good many centuries the lakes were barren, but when the oceans receded the primitive ancestors of present-day cutthroat trout were left behind in the inland sea to the east of the mountains. Trout, among other fish, slowly evolved as the waters receded.

But trout like it cold, and as the water grew warmer they left the huge desert sinks to climb tributary rivers to the higher, cooler basins like the one holding Piute Lake, into which Granite Basin drains. When white men discovered Piute several centuries ago, they found it still brimming with its own native species of speckled trout, despite the fact that Indians who came from the desert every summer netted all they wanted from the tributary streams in woven baskets.

Because of their powerful urge to go upstream, the plentiful Piute trout tried to ascend Granite Creek. The creek-bed climbs very steeply—a thousand feet in less than a mile—through cataracts and falls interspersed with small pools. Several times I have fished my way downstream, past the remains of the Hermit's Hut, past the old powerhouse that once served the Chalet, inspecting every obstacle the Piute trout would have to surmount. It doesn't seem possible that any small fish, jumping upward through a heavy falling torrent, could find the strength to leap so many formidable barriers.

But the trout's determination to go upstream can be incredible. I have often seen trout literally batter themselves to death attempting to climb a cataract they had no chance of ascending. In another range of mountains I once sat for an hour beside a large stream and watched rainbow trout try vainly to jump up a twelve-foot waterfall. Again and again they leaped as much as six feet from the spume, slapped hard against the rock, struggled frantically upward another unbelievable foot or two, then fell back, stunned, to the pool below, where they rested before trying again. In the hour I watched several small fish managed eight or nine feet before falling back. Although the waterfall, to me, seemed utterly impassable, the trout kept on trying, and somehow, I'm sure a few succeeded.

It was probably the same on Granite Creek. Driven by an instinct of astonishing power, a few of the millions of speckled trout that fought their way upstream managed to climb that thousand-foot cascade, and formed the nucleus for what in time became a large trout population in the basin. When the supply of spawning trout in Piute's tributaries dwindled, as white men elbowed out the Indians and organized wholesale slaughter, the Indians followed the trout to Granite Basin.

Early in this century, white men hunting greener fields found Indians netting large quantities of spawning speckled trout from both the channel and Rainbow Creek, and they quickly crowded in to join the harvest. Just as they had at Piute, the speckled trout in Granite began to grow scarce as vulnerable spawners were slaughtered by the thousands. By 1920 they were rarely caught, and ten years later they were gone. In the meantime, a dam had been built at the basin's outlet to increase water storage, and a flume had been constructed around the side of the mountain to divert runoff from eastward flowing Granite Creek into a westward flowing river, where it could generate electricity on its way to irrigate farmlands below.

Now the normal spring and summer runoff flows east to Piute Lake, but in the fall the power company empties the water behind its dam and sends it down the river to the west, lowering the level of Lower Granite five feet. The building of the dam and subsequent raising of the lakes turned the small stream between the lakes into a channel navigable to boats in the summer, permitting cabin construction on Upper Granite. As the speckled trout fishery dwindled to nothing, the Indians who for decades had hunted, trapped, and fished in the basin gradually stopped coming.

German Brown Trout were planted to replace the speckled natives and, being cannibals, probably ate the last of the survivors. Browns grow large and are the smartest of trout. The best way to catch them is to impale a live minnow on a hook and let it swim around in the depths until discovered by a hungry cruising brown. A percentage of these minnows manage to escape both the hook and marauding browns and, being hardy, soon multiply. So the lakes soon became populated with chub, shiners, suckers and red sided minnows—all brought up from the lowlands by anglers pursuing big browns.

As fishing pressure grew the Department of Fish and Game (DFG), in an effort to provide more sport, began planting large numbers of rainbow trout fingerlings. But fishing failed to improve because the minnows both outhustled the baby rainbows for food and outbred them, while the cannibal browns ate everything in sight. Despairing of establishing a sport fishery as long as browns ruled the waters, the DFG decided to poison the lakes and start over. Early one fall, as soon as the water level was

down for the winter, they laced both lakes liberally with rotenone, which quickly suffocates all fish life by attacking the
nervous system.

Within a few days the surface was churning with gasping,
dying fish of all sizes and breeds. The sight was both terrible and
fascinating. For the first and only time it was possible to see the
basin's entire fish population. There were very few big browns,
millions of minnows, and a surprisingly large number of rainbows, including some large ones. Jorgy took a boat through the
shoals of dying fish, selectively netting rainbows, which he
cleaned and packaged and stored in his freezer. Rotenone has no
effect upon humans, nor does it affect the taste or edibility of
trout. On winter patrol that year I ate quite a number, and they
were excellent.

Within three or four days of the poisoning, every fish in the
basin was dead. Two weeks later when we returned to the cabin,
our cove was half filled with bloated, rotting, fungus-covered
fish brought down the lake by the dependable west wind. Every
foot of shore at our end of the lake was heaped with putrifying
fish, and the smell was overpowering. We only stayed one night.
Fortunately the fall was warm throughout October, causing
most of the fish to decompose completely before winter set in.
The following spring the fish were gone but the poison that
killed them was another matter.

The rotenone dosage was supposed to be just large enough to
ensure that all fish at all depths were killed. The chemical was to
dissipate or break down long before the spring thaw could raise
the lakes enough to wash it down Granite Creek to the trout-
inhabited river below. But there was either a gross miscalcula-
tion or the overkill margin was set far too high, and clearly the
DFG hadn't thought about heavy fall rainstorms. After a balmy
October, it rained so hard in November that the lake quickly
rose and Granite Creek again began to flow.

Almost at once trout started dying by the thousands in the
river below. Gasping rainbows and browns clotted every pool all
the way to Piute Lake, outraging anglers and residents. The
DFG rushed a pair of fishery biologists to Granite Basin with a
supply of the chlorine compound that would neutralize the
rotenone flowing down the creek. When the rain turned to

snow, the DFG had just enough time to bring its men a house-trailer before deep drifts closed the road for the winter.

Unfortunately, the chlorine was also highly toxic to trout and had to be kept to a fairly precise concentration to prevent the death of even more fish. It proved to be a difficult winter of tropical storms interspersed with hard freezes and deep snows. The biologists could not afford to leave their post. I remember how forlorn they looked, trudging from their almost buried trailer to the garbage platform where the chlorine was kept, then down through the drifts to the icy stream, where they metered out the neutralizing chemical.

The following summer, to the DFG's continuing embarrassment, the concentration of rotenone in both lakes was still too high to plant fish, although the downstream crisis was past. A year later, with the poison finally gone, the basin was stocked with vast numbers of rainbow fingerlings, a few thousand catchable-sized rainbows as a peace offering to anglers, two hundred large rainbows for breeding purposes, and hundreds of thousands of tiny kokanee salmon. The salmon were supposed to provide added sport while not directly competing with the rainbows for food.

Five years later, despite annual plantings, the lakes were yielding few fish and the grumblings were growing louder. Growth in the rainbows was painfully slow, and kokanee were almost never caught. The DFG claimed the basin was deficient in natural food—despite the large fish populations of the past—and insisted the poisoning was in no way responsible for the poor performance of its planted fish. But in response to complaints it planted fresh water shrimp, and within a few years Granite trout began to grow, and their flesh, which had been white, turned salmon pink.

The salmon, however, have proved to be a tragic mistake. Rapid multiplication has restricted their growth as well as that of the trout, for while their diets are not identical there is a sizeable area of overlap. The little kokanee lie deep, breeding and eating, their numbers growing steadily since few of them are caught. Fishermen who regularly troll the lakes for rainbow say the salmon often strike but the hooks rip loose from their delicate mouths before they can be landed.

Fifteen years have passed since the rotenone experiment, and fishing for rainbow remains only fair. The voracious salmon continue to accumulate, and now that the suckers and minnows are gone, algae and aquatic plants are growing on the lake bottom. Some people think suckers should be reintroduced to control aquatic plant growth, a suggestion that horrifies the DFG. Others would submit to another dose of poison to get rid of proliferating salmon, alarming those who are convinced the lakes have yet to recover from the first disastrous experiment. At present, no change is expected.

* * *

It's hard to keep track of trout in the winter, but I often ski across the upper lake to see if kokanee are lying in the open water at the mouth of Rainbow Creek, and whenever I go to the channel for water I always check the ice-free pools in hopes of spotting a foraging rainbow. As I tramp across the ice, I sometimes shudder to think of the thousands of fish lying torpid in the dark freezing water beneath me, and I wonder if they feel the vibrations of my footsteps. Now and then I hear of anglers who have sawed through the ice to fish the bottom with bait, and some have made good catches, but I have never been tempted.

As lengthening winter days begin to melt the snow, the channel becomes a torrent that gouges a pool in the lower lake ice pack. The water glitters and hisses with dissolving ice, and miniature icebergs bob in the eddies. One warm day in late April I was sitting on a boulder close to the water, listening to the thunder, when I thought I saw the flash of a turning trout on the edge of the current. I hurried back to the cabin across the snow for my fly rod, and returned to float a dusty grey hackle down the current.

To my great surprise, a nice brook trout rose deliberately on the third or fourth cast, snapped at the fly and missed, then turned to pursue it and was hooked. He fought very little, like a nearly spent spawner, before allowing himself to be beached. There was nothing in his stomach but a single large ant, and it's hard to imagine where he found it.

Two years later, almost to the day, the pool looked so inviting that I again made a trip for my fly rod. This time I landed a small rainbow right away, and again saw no sign of other fish.

After that, fishing the pool at the mouth of the channel a month or more before the ice went out became something of a ritual. Never have I managed to raise—or even see—another fish, but the hope remains, and if the weather is right it is always a pleasure to cast a fly again on moving water.

Late in the spring when the ice is breaking up, I find it hard to stay away from the channel. The current is swift, the holes are bottle green, and ice floes float downstream to crunch against boulders and run aground in the shallows. Dimly heard beneath the water's rush is the deep, hollow grinding and bumping of rocks on the bottom. One June day, in our second year in the basin, I was walking up the channel toward the cabin, thinking of the long list of jobs that needed doing, when I stopped to peer down into the deep gravel hollow spawning rainbows like best. Wind and current conspired to keep the surface opaque, and I started to leave because there were screens to put up and shutters to take down, but then I stopped because I hadn't found out if the spawners had come, and it was something I wanted to know. I sat down on the grass and fixed my attention on the swirling green water, waiting for the surface to clear. The flashing light, and continuous motion enveloped me. So did the soft rushing sound and changing color. Birds flashed across the water, a butterfly fluttered in the shrubbery close beside me, a ladybug fearlessly crawled up my arm.

I sank deeper in the grass, totally absorbed, feeling the penetrating warmth of the sun. I sighed and felt my muscles relaxing. I yawned and felt tension subsiding. In the hypnotizing spell of the river I was relaxed as though for sleep yet alert to my surroundings, cut off from the world beyond my view. I felt light as a bird, still as a stone, as free as rising smoke, and as supple as a river spreading out in a lake. It must have been an hour that I sat beside the channel, watching fruitlessly for trout, before the spell released me and I got to my feet and slowly walked on to the cabin.

In the years just after the sterile lakes were restocked, the big mature rainbows that had been planted for seed, guided by instinct, moved up into the channel's current to spawn in the gravel of the deep middle pool. It was difficult at first to see exactly what was happening, but hours of observation enabled me to piece together a picture. I watched entranced as trout two feet in length split into pairs, selected nest sites, then scooped out the gravel with powerful thrusts of their tails. The female sank deep in the nest to lay eggs, then the male settled down to cover them with fertilizing milt.

Unfortunately, neither spawners nor spawn were left in peace. After the long winter upper lakers are eager to get up the channel to their cabins, and back-country travelers clamor for taxi service to the upper lake trailhead. So once the channel is navigable, the rush is on. Standing on shore in those early years, I watched terrified spawners racing madly to escape each motorboat coming up the channel. When a boat was gone the trout were still nervous, restlessly milling for five or ten minutes before returning to the gravel. Once the channel was open to boats, the number of spawners declined every day, and inside of a week the last of them were gone. It might be, of course, that the fish had finished spawning, but I landed spawners a week or two later while casting from my pier, suggesting that the fish had been driven prematurely from their nests.

Even if the spawning process had been completed I wonder how many of the tender eggs survived. How resistant could they be to the poisonous exhaust fumes pumped into the water by every passing motorboat, mine included? Then there was the unburned gasoline and motor oil that is spilled in the lake in such liberal quantities that the lakes are marked by a black oily band at high water. Some of that pollutant surely settled into the gravel of the channel's spawning beds.

Conditions in the channel got steadily worse for the trout as the season progressed. Motorboat travel continued to increase as the weather grew hotter, and when all the snow was gone the surface water warmed and the flow through the channel grew progressively slower. Conditions were probably at their worst in mid-August when trout fry were scheduled to emerge from their eggs. If any survived, I never saw one.

The spectacle of big rainbows spawning in the channel did not last. The situation was artificial. The trout I saw were a remnant of the two hundred seed fish planted in the hope that natural reproduction might supplement the annual plant of fingerling rainbows. In that sense they were only an experiment, and one that apparently failed. When they died of old age after three or four years there were none to replace them.

It has been nearly ten years since the last of those seedfish came into the channel to spawn. A few big trout, grown from planted fingerlings, are caught now each year, so the fishery is maturing, but they make no attempt to spawn in the channel.

Being an admirer—as well as a catcher—of trout, I have always been interested in widening their distribution. Water takes on an added allure when it supports a population of trout. One winter day while studying a map, I realized I knew several sterile lakes in the wilderness back of Granite Basin that would probably support trout. Why not plant them, and perhaps produce some good fishing? Old timers, I knew, had often stocked barren waters by carrying a coffee pot full of trout from one drainage to the next. For me, the job should be easier. I could purchase or trap enough small trout to fill my five-gallon plastic jug, lash the jug to a packframe and carry it back to a fishless lake.

I decided on a cold, deep, well-hidden little tarn well away from the trails and forgotten on the maps. Rainbow might well spawn in either of the two inlet streams fed by shaded snowfields. Excited by the project, I began to hunt for trout before summer began. Fish stores, I quickly learned, cannot deal in game fish, and trout farms will not sell less than a hundred pounds of live trout at a time. I visited a "U-Catchem" trout pond fifteen miles away at Piute Lake and explained in vague terms what I wanted to do. The proprietor said he would sell me as many fish as I wanted for a dollar apiece, but I would have to accept whatever he netted, and the fish would run eight or nine inches, at least. He hoped I wouldn't have to carry them far because six fish that big would need at least three gallons of cold water in a five-gallon can, and the water would have to be constantly stirred to maintain enough oxygen to keep the fish alive. What I really ought to have, he said dryly, were fingerlings.

That was sobering news. If what he said was true, it would be hard enough to keep fingerlings healthy on a five-mile walk, half of it cross-country, on a warm summer day. On my way back to

Granite I bought a wire mesh minnow trap with inward pointing cones at each end. At the cabin I baited it with meat scraps as suggested in the instructions, and hung it in a shady place underneath the pier. The instructions promised half a dozen minnows would arrive within hours, but to ensure a full trap it was best to leave it undisturbed overnight. I restrained myself from looking until the following morning, but the trap was perfectly empty.

Remembering the meat was marinated, I switched to dry bread, also guaranteed as "sure-fire" in the instructions, but the following morning the trap was still empty. Deciding the raisins in the bread were at fault, I substituted dough balls made from scraps of piecrust, the last bait suggested in the instructions. When that failed, it dawned on me that minnows and fingerlings aren't the same thing. Minnows are what were poisoned in order to plant fingerling trout. The absence of fingerlings might be explained by the big trout that hang around the dock. Maybe what I needed was sheltered water.

That night after dark I quietly beached the canoe at the mouth of Rainbow Creek in the middle of the Scout camp and slipped upstream with my trap to the bridge. Before the trap could be baited and set, I heard voices approaching down the path. Hoping the darkness and the bridge would conceal me, I crouched down and froze. Footsteps stopped just above my head and an adolescent voice demanded "What're you doing down there, kid?"

"Kid!" I said indignantly. "What do you mean, kid?" It was all I could think of, but it seemed to be enough. The boy hastily apologized and continued on his way, but not before his flashlight beam paused on my trap. When he was gone I moved upstream to another location and carefully concealed the trap underwater, leaving with considerable misgivings. It wasn't hard to imagine a Scout treasure hunt the next morning. But when I returned the next night the trap was still there—and still empty.

Remembering small trout in the Granite Creek pools below the dam, I took my trap down behind the Chalet. Baiting it this time with raw meat and bits of cheese, I sank it beneath the

willows in a fishy looking pool. When I cautiously raised it the
following day I was astonished to find three five-inch trout.
Lowering it back in place, I returned to the cabin to build a
holding tank in which to stockpile my catch beneath the pier.
That afternoon when I returned to the trap I was delighted to
find the catch had grown to five. In two or three days I should
have the dozen rainbows I needed.

I emptied the trap into my carrying pail, but two little trout
leapt back into the brook before I could clamp on the lid.
Rebaiting the trap, I sank it deep in a good pool downstream and
took my first three fish to the holding tank. In the next two days
I caught four more trout, and with seven finning quietly under
the pier prospects looked good. But the following three days
were not only unproductive, two of the fish in the holding tank
died.

A visit to the trap, in the last good looking pool, revealed two
trout caught, but when I returned to collect them hours later,
both trout and trap had disappeared! And when I got home, two
more trout in the holding tank were dead. With only three trout
left and no trap, I resigned myself to buying from the U-Catchem pond after all.

With a hand-operated air mattress pump and a big, lidded
bucket I returned to the trout pond, where the proprietor's
teenage son was on duty, and asked for a half-dozen of the
smallest rainbows he could net. The challenge appealed to him,
as it did to the handful of loungers who were watching. Soon
four of us were sprinkling trout chow on water madly boiling
with fish, all shouting to call the boy's attention to a particularly
small trout. He would scoop up a netful of squirming fish and
yell "Are any of these small enough to keep?" Most of them
seemed huge, ten or twelve inches, but now and then a smaller
one appeared and got dumped in my bucket, where one of the
loungers was blowing bubbles with the air mattress pump.

After fifteen hectic minutes there were an undetermined
number of eight to ten inch rainbows racing madly in the bucket,
and it seemed like time to quit. At the U-Catchem shack the
boy's grandfather insisted the fish must be counted and measured to determine their value. That would kill the already

overstimulated trout, I protested—pumping all the while—and begged them to take a guess at the total price. When agreement was reached I wrestled the sloshing bucket into the car in front of the passenger seat, gave the pump a few quick squeezes and drove away.

As I cruised toward the basin, pumping several times a minute, I noted that the frenzy in the bucket was subsiding. Then all at once a trout leapt out of the water and flopped back in the bucket. "Hey," I yelled, "Cut that out!" A minute later a second trout jumped, bounced off the dashboard and fell back in the water. The lid wouldn't stay on the bucket because of the pump, and I cursed each time a fish leapt, imagining the damage to the slippery mucus coating that protects them from fungus.

On a hairpin turn as the car climbed toward the pass, water sloshed from the bucket and an opportunistic nine-incher jumped free, bouncing off the gear shift and flopping on the floor at my feet. Afraid to lose another, I gave a dozen fierce pumps, yanked the pump from the water, jammed the lid on the bucket and floorboarded the car. In three minutes' time I reached the marina, and fifteen minutes later the fish were safely shut in the holding tank under the pier. They milled excitedly for several minutes, then settled down at different depths in parallel formation, pointing upwind. They seemed perfectly tranquil, but I was ready for a drink! Freda came to look and suggested we keep them, "so we can have trout for dinner whenever we want."

My collection, I felt sure, would benefit from a day of rest before another exciting trip. Besides there were more preparations to be made. I lashed the white plastic five-gallon jug to a packframe, taped the pump's air hose to a straightened wire coathanger, and filled all of the refrigerator's ice trays. Then I made arrangements with Megan and Amy, the sisters who had offered to come along and pump.

They met me on the pier after breakfast two days later and we completed preparations. When all the fish had been transferred from the tank to the jug, we emptied in the ice cubes and added enough water to make a cargo of close to four gallons. The nozzle of the pump was pushed to the bottom of the tank and Megan went to work on the bellows, sending air bubbles spraying among the milling trout. After motoring up the lake to the trailhead, I climbed into the pack, fastened the waistbelt and started up the trail, with one of the sisters following close behind me, pumping.

Carrying an open jug containing 30 pounds of water and a small school of fish, I soon discovered, was a disconcerting experience. The load seemed to move with a life of its own. When I leaned to the right there was a moment's hesitation, then a strong surge would shove me off balance as the water caught up. Added to this imbalance were occasional backward tugs from the sister attached by the umbilical cord of the pump.

All this uncontrolled motion kept water sloshing out through the necessarily open mouth of the jug. It ran down my back, into my shorts, then down my legs and into my boots. From time to time we stopped so one of the sisters could peer into the tank and give me a progress report: "There's one upside down! Wait. Now he's right side up. When the water quiets down they look all right."

Whenever we passed another party on the trail, I was acutely aware of the gurgling and splashing and how odd we must look. We'd offer brief greetings and hurry past, as though late for an urgent rendezvous.

"After we passed," a sister would report, "they turned around and stared." It was the same with every encounter, but no one was rude enough to ask what we were up to. Because of the dubious legality of this highly irregular planting, Amy went ahead whenever we approached a place where rangers might be waiting to ask embarrassing questions. It was with considerable relief that I finally left the trail for the cross-country portion of the trip.

The water sloshing down my back gradually reduced the level in the jug, and after an hour we found it necessary to stop at every lake or stream to add a quart or two with the plastic bottle we had brought along for making lemonade. Then the pump began to fail, the slightest tug causing it to part from the tube inside the jug. Fortunately, Megan had slim wrists and could reach down among the trout to retrieve and reconnect it. Half a mile from the lake the pump gave up completely, and there was nothing to do but pick up the pace and hope they had air enough to last.

101

When at last we reached the lakeshore I stripped off the pack and dumped it, frame and all, in the water. Fish are sensitive, I know, to sudden changes in temperature, and the water in the jug, after traveling two hours, must have been considerably warmer than the lake. After a minute or two of worrying about the oxygen supply, I sank the jug to the bottom, allowing it to fill, and waited for the trout to swim gratefully away. They didn't. So I lifted the jug, turned it upside down and poured. Reluctantly, the trout splashed into the lake with the last of the water.

To my pleasure and surprise every fish seemed healthy and alert. At first they found it hard to believe they weren't confined. They moved a few inches, stopped, then moved a little farther. Finding no obstruction their runs became longer, and in less than a minute the last of them had left the shallow inlet and disappeared into the aquamarine depths. The job was done.

I hugged my faithful pumpers, spread my socks and jacket in the sun to dry, and we sat down for lunch on the grassy shore. As we ate I wondered how my fish would fare in their new home. Insects were plentiful in the willow by the water, and polywogs wriggled in the shallows. Food would be ample and three months of mild weather should give them time to fatten and learn their surroundings before the first ice began to form. But the low winter sun would not reach this sheltered bowl, and the ice might last seven or eight months. Winter would be long and dark for my trout. Would they survive it?

I wish I could report that when I returned, eleven months later, a dozen rainbows were contentedly frisking in the shallows. Though I spent an hour walking the shore, peering into the depths, waiting for a rise, I saw no sign of fish. The lake seemed lonely and desolate. I cast a barbless fly in the shade beneath the willows, but no curious trout rose to inspect it. Still, I have hope that the fish survived and may yet multiply to populate the lake.

SEVEN

Granite Garden

I never cease to be amazed that anything grows on the scoured granite shores of Granite Lakes. During the half year that is winter the basin is buried deep in snow and for the nearly rainless summer and fall, dry winds parch the land. Yet the half-acre surrounding the cabin is transformed each spring into an alpine garden before the last of the winter snow is gone. The first flowers are blooming before the ice goes out, and even in late fall, after months without rain, blossoms are still to be found in sheltered nooks.

The garden, though untended, yields great variety in surprisingly rapid succession. There is no time to waste. With three seasons to be crowded into only four months, each plant must grow to maturity, flower, and ripen its fruit before the smothering snow returns. I'm no naturalist, but over the years I've learned to measure the advance of the seasons by the changes in the several dozen grasses, plants, shrubs, and trees that grow around the cabin.

Only moments ago, geologically speaking, the latest in a series of glaciers dug up and carried off the last remnants of the basin's topsoil, exposing the granite bedrock buried for ages deep in the earth. When the ice receded before a warming climate, all that remained was a boulder-studded bowl of monolithic granite strewn with shattered rock, gravel, and glacial flour—all ground by the mill of moving ice, all of it barren of life-supporting nutrients. Even the blowing dust was sterile.

Ten thousand years have passed since then, but the change in the land has been slight. Granite Lakes now fill the scoured granite bowl, but more than half the land that surrounds them is much the way the glaciers left it—naked and barren granite incapable of supporting life, except for primitive lichens. On the peninsula between the lakes where the cabin sits, rounded boulders still stand where they were stranded by the ice. Sculpted slabs and granite domes still show scratches and grooves that point down the basin along the path of long-departed ice, and remnants of glacier polish still shine in the sunlight.

But over the years the rock has weathered and cracked. Seeds and spores, bacteria and pollen have arrived on the wind and settled in the cracks, along with sand and dust, to offer enterprising plants a modest foothold. Today in the hollows and cracks in the granite there are shallow pockets of inferior soil, its principal ingredients gravel, dust, decayed wood and grasses, pine pollen, and needles.

This sad soil is buried from December through May by an annual snowfall of thirty to forty feet. In the spring it is flooded and eroded by torrents of snowmelt water. In the almost rainless summer it gradually grows parched in the unfiltered high-altitude sunlight and intermittent dry winds—winds that blow away the finest, lightest materials. Though snow commonly falls in every month of the year, rain is scarce. Three or four months may pass with scarcely a drop, and the drought of summer and fall often ends with snow, not badly needed rain.

Before the snow is gone in spring, wildlife is busily at work in the soil. Moles, gophers, and ground squirrels riddle it with tunnels. The heavy population of summer nesting birds keeps the ground well-plucked of worms and insects. With the help of grazing rodents and rock rabbits, the birds keep it shorn of delectable grasses. In the course of a year, surface temperatures may vary a hundred degrees. Winds occasionally reach a hundred miles an hour. Nevertheless, these patches of poor soil somehow support a remarkably varied and luxuriant vegetation.

The land surrounding the cabin ranges from bare rock to swamp, and the plants it supports are just as varied. Contrast frequently is sharp, since wet and dry sites are often only inches apart. The total area is small. From the upper lake shoreline to the channel pool is less than fifty yards. But within that short distance one encounters gravel ledges, a grassy flat, an intermit-

tent stream, glacially smoothed slab culminating in small domes, small cliffs, a lush patch of marsh, and the rocky peninsula leading to the channel. This is the terrain on which our garden grows each spring.

When it comes to keeping pace with the swiftly passing seasons, no plant outperforms the mountain ash, which grows as a shrub, not a tree, in the mountains of the west. A sizable clump grows at the base of the bluff at the back of the cove. After observing its continually changing form for fifteen years, I can almost tell time by the stage of its development. If it were not for the sheltering roots of a neighboring lodgepole pine, the few inches of soil in which the ash lives would long since have washed away. Waves break all summer against the shrub's exposed roots, and when the wind blows hard the drenched foliage is flattened back against the cliff.

In winter, snow blown down the lake by the prevailing winds drifts ten to fifteen feet deep at the foot of the cliff. When the ice goes out in Upper Granite, sometime between mid-May and mid-June, often the ash is still buried beneath the remains of this drift. Before bare ground begins to show by the shore, blood-red stalks that have sprouted in the dark beneath the snow spring erect through the slush into sunlight.

A few days of heat swell bulging buds which erupt within a week into a series of tiny, pale propeller blades, each of which opens like a fan to produce eleven to thirteen leaflets. At the base of each unfolding leaf, less than two weeks from its emergence from the snow, the swiftly growing plant produces a tiny grapelike cluster that will later unfold into blossom. Flowers often begin to mature on sunny upper branches while the lower stems are still struggling to rise through the last of the wet, heavy snow.

By the time snow has disappeared from the shore sometime in June, the lacy network of tender red branches is two feet high and four feet across. Inside it, the flattened grey skeleton of last year's bush is still plainly visible. By mid- to late June, only a month emerged from the snow, the ash is half again as large and thickening foliage hides the decomposing stalks of the previous year. And the tiny bunch of green grapes has opened into a flat-topped cluster of eighty to two hundred half-inch white flowers.

Most years the blossom cluster is fading by the fourth of July, and by the middle of the month the persistent wind has scattered most of the wilted white petals. As the flowers disappear, the growing fruits beneath them stand revealed for the first time, clusters of green BB shot that look remarkably like the grapelike blossom clusters that preceded them. By mid-August, as summer begins to fade, the BBs have grown to the size of peas and half of them are tinted pink like ripening apples, while here and there in the lush green foliage occasional leaves have prematurely turned red or gold.

Autumn in Granite Basin usually begins in late August or early September, and the ash always heralds the season's change. All at once the pink-green berries are a shiny Chinese red, and fully half the leaves have turned yellow or strawberry pink. The change occurs overnight and requires no catalyst of frost. Unlike most autumn foliage, the deep green on the mountain ash does not fade when red and yellow appear. On one branch of eleven leaflets, three may be dark green, three red and green, three pure red, and two all yellow.

As September passes into October and nights slip below freezing, the green leaves diminish and the yellow multiply. But even after the first snows there are a few green leaves to be found. The upstanding clusters of red berries undergo no change at all during September and October. Apparently the bitter pulp has no appeal to birds and squirrels. In November, when snows may last a week before melting, the ash is a bright cloud of color against the snow-whitened background—its leaves now mostly yellow, some edged in red, a few deep maroon and rare ones still green. Waiting for winter it hovers motionless above a growing carpet of yellow and brown leaves, its bright berry clusters still intact, its upright stems blood red.

Then in December the snow comes often and stays. Like a gallant captain on the bridge of a sinking ship, the ash is engulfed by the drifting snow that will bury it for the next half year.

Even before the first shoots of mountain ash poke through the spring snow, Douglas phlox is blooming twenty feet above it atop the hot granite bluff. Snow depth makes the big difference. The same wind that piles deep drifts at the edge of the cove keeps the bluff top bare for probably half the winter. By the end of April, winter snow is gone and the surface of the bluff's rocky soil is warm and dry.

Even in early spring, surrounded by snow, the grey-green foliage and bare shaggy bark of the phlox give it a dry, dusty look. The wiry, woody little plant forms a creeping prickly mat on dry rocky sites. Like its companion the juniper, it disdains shelter, water, and decent soil, choosing to grow only on arid windy slopes. Give it a decent home and it surely will die.

Though the plant is usually scraggly and chooses barren sites, its blossoms are delicate and profuse. Most are pure white, but there are always clumps of flowers tinged with lavender and pink. These first blossoms of the year are a welcome sight, confirming that summer is just a week or two away.

The largest shrubs in my garden are the water-loving willows. Along with alder, they dominate the strip of swamp that fronts the channel, and there are four large clumps near the cabin. Spears of new growth emerge through the snow as early as May, and fuzzy pussy willows wave fresh tassels in the spring wind even before the ash is ready to flower. One clump grows from

107

the base of a long-dead pine at the mouth of the cove, and always manages to block the path to the pier by August.

As summer advances, a still larger clump invades the back porch. Like its neighbor ten feet away, it was a modest little bush until our hundred-gallon sump for wash water was dug halfway between the two plants and covered over. Since then the pair have gone wild, doubling in size every year. At their current rate of growth they'll engulf the garden in another few years. I try not to think what their roots are doing to the sump.

Next in size to the willows are the thickets of huckleberry oak. But unlike the annual and deciduous willow, the waist-high oak is evergreen and perennial. Winter snows crush its wiry branches flat but they spring back once the load is lifted. In fact shrubs beneath deep snow fare better than those on top of the bluffs. Foliage exposed to winter winds invariably turns brown and dies before spring. By the time the huckleberry oak has shaken off the drifts of spring snow there is already two inches of tender jade growth at the end of each grey-green branch.

The first grasses emerge as soon as bare spots appear in the snow, and they thrive in the hot sun of long days and the continual irrigation provided by melting snow. New grass is always in great demand among nest-building birds and famished ground squirrels. Together they keep it cropped short for weeks.

Right behind the wiry phlox comes what I call "beet" buckwheat. Three or four different buckwheats grow in our garden. This one has a small pompon of tiny white blossoms that unfolds in June from a blood-red bud. Waving at the end of long bare stems, the blooms seem to last half the summer. Wrinkled glossy leaves with purple veins and stems remind me of beet foliage. Like the phlox, beet buckwheat likes dry, rocky soil and unsheltered sites, but it has a much greater range. Besides growing on the bluff, it sprouts from all the cracks and pockets of soil among the slabs and domes behind the cabin.

By the end of June in an average year, plants of all sorts are showing signs of life. The woody branches of last year's penstemon, squashed flat by the snow, are sprouting green branchlets, the dead-looking clumps of spirea are sending out pink shoots, and turquoise leaves are unfolding on the serviceberry.

These three intermingle in the larger pockets of slightly better
soil beneath the trees along the margins of the domes.

Fifty yards up the draw from the outhouse is a snowmelt pool
about forty yards long, fifteen yards wide, and two feet deep.
Shaded by steep bluffs and surrounding trees, it holds snow and
ice until late in June and forms a reservoir for the stream that
flows past the outhouse, under the cabin and out across the lawn
to the lake. In the sheltered draw in early season the moss is
lush and three different ferns—rockcress, rockbrake and grape-
fern—begin to unfold their prehistoric-looking fronds. This
damp pocket of shady luxuriance lies no more than fifteen feet
from the bare windy home of the drought-loving phlox.

Before June is gone I begin to look for two of my favorite
plants: golden brodiaea and streptanthus. Brodiaea is easy to
miss. The graceful golden blossom, darkly etched along the
veins like a spotted tiger lily, is less than an inch across and
stands on a bare stem only four inches high. It blooms for
perhaps a week, then utterly disappears. No trace of the little
plant remains by mid-July. In our backyard the brodiaea (growing best beneath the hammock) is too rare to pick, but when I
walk where it grows thickly I pluck it from the ground as the
Indians used to and eat the sweet tuber.

If brodiaea is the prettiest plant in the garden, streptanthus is
easily the most exotic. Imagine a curved ten-inch stem which
seems to skewer encircling leaves that come in a variety of
different shapes. Bright purple blossoms hanging gracefully at
the end of each stem contrast strikingly with delicate yellow-
green leaves. Streptanthus first appears before the end of June
and can still occasionally be found in late August, when its
flowers have been replaced by six-inch, scythe-like seed pods.
In the garden it grows best in the shallow draw around the old
incinerator.

July is the month when most flowers bloom. Sulphur flower,
probably the showiest of the buckwheats, is usually flowering by
the Fourth in the gravel below the bluff and around the backyard domes. Clumps of stiff six-inch stems rise from a mat of
thick leathery jade-colored leaves to dense clusters of yellow
blossoms. These golden pompons lose none of their petals when

109

picked and dried. There's a bouquet in a bottle that's been sitting on one of the cabin's windowsills now for five years.

When it comes to color, mountain penstemon produces more than all the other flowers combined. The mats of tiny saw-toothed leaves are unobtrusive in June, but when the blossoms open in early July the two-inch scarlet trumpets seem to cover the ground beneath the trees.

Before the last of them have shriveled, the dusty pink pom-pons of spirea come into bloom around the back porch and in a gravel flat halfway to the outhouse. Spirea can't match the gaudy penstemon in brilliance, but the flowers last three times as long, often past the middle of August. And when the flowers fade and disappear in the wind, its delicate saw-toothed leaves turn brief-ly red, then translucent gold.

The miniature sunflower called groundsel or ragwort appears in early July where the sun is brightest. Even in full bloom it has a straggly, ravaged look, with one or two petals usually missing, but the bright yellow blossoms somehow last at least a month. The sticky stem attracts all manner of bugs, and the long triangu-lar leaves make me think of mint.

Penstemon and spirea are the champion bloomers, but right behind comes creambush or creamberry. A big patch against the bluff beneath the kitchen window turns white with small blos-soms as early as late June and is often still blooming at the end of August. In fact, nothing in the garden blooms longer. I particu-larly like the deep green leaves which are toothed and fluted like tiny fans. Only creamberry dares to grow in the cracks on the windy waterfront bluff that even the hardy phlox disdains.

Late one July I was surprised to discover the rose-purple blossoms of swamp onion growing in the cracks of the domes and slabs. The onion is supposed to be a gangly plant growing three feet high in wet mountain meadows. Here it grows no more than three inches high in hot, dry sand. I pulled a tuber from the ground and tasted it. Onion, without a doubt. Never have I found them growing in the swamp, only twenty feet away, where they belong.

In August the garden begins to fade. Three or four grasses and sedges stay green and the lawn by the lake stands tall and rank, but the early grasses turn to tangled blond tufts and most of the flowers are withered or past their prime. Still, there are a few plants yet to bloom. A spot of lilac in the rock slide across the cove signals the unfolding of fireweed's tall blossoms. (I never see them without remembering the hundreds of miles of the Alaska Highway which they line.) The only other place in the garden they care to grow is in the shady center of a locked stand of dwarf lodgepole pine in the swamp, a strange place for sun-loving plants.

On the edge of the swamp by the channel pool grow several bushy clumps of Labrador tea. Delicate drooping white flowers of this evergreen hang over the water from branches tipped with tassels of leathery, yellow-green leaves. The plant is graceful, not unlike an azalea, but the tea it makes tastes terrible.

Sometime after the middle of August a groundcover of rubbery, white-veined leaves at the base of several trees near the lawn sends up stems hooked at the end like shepherds' crooks. Heather-like green and white bells grow only on the inside of the stems. Just last summer a knowledgeable neighbor identified the little plant as a member of the wintergreen family, and she insisted that, being evergreen, it must be green all winter beneath the snow. I hope to remember to dig down and look.

I keep an eye out every August for a solitary plant of swamp whitehead (or ranger's button) that rises from the tall grass in the center of the lawn beside a slim lodgepole. The fuzzy white pompons, each on a long stem, somehow amuse me. Perhaps it's the thought of how funny they'd look on a ranger's uniform shirt.

If flowers are scarce in August, fruits and berries are not. The Chinese-red berry clusters of the mountain ash can be found in the swamp, as well as on the bush at the edge of the cove. And there is one tenacious ash that comes up year after year in the middle of the path to the dock between two trees. It takes a terrible beating from passing feet and always looks bedraggled by the end of summer, but it stubbornly persists and I can't bring myself to remove it.

The serviceberry produces big juicy blue berries, twice the size of blueberries, but the birds and squirrels don't like them much. I don't blame them, although Indians and early trappers are supposed to have eaten them.

I used to think that the clump of creek dogwood under the

front porch sprouted a crop of red berries in August, but then I remembered seeing white berries in July. The berry-like spots of red, like single salmon eggs, turned out to be swellings in the margins of occasional leaves. They appear every year and seem to cause no harm, but they must represent a parasite of sorts.

In late August the clusters of berries on the solitary gooseberry bush near the outhouse are still small and hard, with only a rosy hint of their future redness. Juniper berries, like dusty purple-black grapes, have reached full size by the end of summer, but it will be several months before the birds find them ripe enough to eat. The little acorns of the huckleberry oak do not ripen until their second autumn, but the ground squirrels begin harvesting late in summer, so all we ever see are empty shells.

When September arrives summer is gone, and so are almost all the blooms in our garden. Creamberry and scattered white buckwheat are still in blossom, but most of the color comes from rust and gold spirea foliage, blond shining tufts of dead grass, and, of course, the mountain ash with its clumps of red berries and red and yellow leaves. Even before the first cold nights, the willow thickets fade to soft yellow and begin to lose their leaves. One September I was surprised to discover in the swamp's deepest shade a solitary sprig of meadow goldenrod. Elsewhere in the basin I know where to find scarlet gilia, tiger lilies, pussy paws, and other late bloomers lasting well into autumn, but for the most part fall means the flowers are gone.

My favorite fall flora is probably alpine laurel. Like wintergreen it's supposed to be evergreen, but it usually doesn't appear until early September. In a windswept patch of soil near the pier it reaches a height of only two inches, but in the more protected swamp it sometimes grows several feet high. I rarely notice it in either place until the translucent leaves turn strawberry red and glow vividly when backlighted by the low autumn sun.

The only other plant to appear in the fall is the first stage of the exotic streptanthus, better known for its stem encircling foliage in July. These little leafy rosettes lying flat on the ground make possible next summer's purple-flowering plants.

The biggest part of any garden is its trees, and thanks to an abundance of water near the cabin we are well stocked, even if nearly all of them are lodgepole pine. A dozen tall ones grow out of the lawn, half a dozen more rise close to the cabin in the incinerator draw, and a dense forest of smaller trees grows down the creek from the snowpool and around the outhouse. A pair of mighty specimens rise just beyond the domes to frame my view of Eagle Peak, and a tangled, impenetrable thicket of saplings forms the heart of the swamp.

The lodgepoles make their presence felt early every summer. By the end of June, yellow blossoms dot the tip of each dark green branchlet. Then in early July the swollen pollen sacs surrounding each flower literally explode, broadcasting yellow dust everywhere. On windy days the basin's air actually glows yellow. So does the lake where a thick band of yellow water rings the shore, and rocks are encrusted with thick yellow scum. For two or three weeks the dread dust is everywhere, and naturally it gets blamed for maladies of all sorts, from asthma to hay fever to stomach flu. Finally, by late July the last of the pollen sacs have emptied, the yellow ring around the lake has sunk, persistent wind has cleared the air, and Granite Lakers have stopped sneezing. The pollen deluge is over for another year.

A pair of sixty foot lodgepoles used to grow in the water beside the pier near the cove. I returned one spring to find their water-rotted roots had snapped in a winter storm and the trees, still alive, had fallen downwind toward the cabin, their tops coming to rest not ten feet from the cabin's biggest window. That was before the fireplace was built, so when a neighbor offered to buck them up in exchange for half the wood, I readily agreed. He started at the top, methodically sawing off twenty-inch rounds. When he reached a point ten feet from the upthrust roots, their weight suddenly overbalanced the shortened trunk and the tree shot upright, nearly taking the sawyer with it. To finish the job, he had to fall two ten-foot stumps!

Three of my favorite lodgepoles are dead but still standing. Their shaggy bark is gone, leaving satin-smooth columns of bone-white wood. They gleam like shafts of ivory among the honey and green of their living neighbors, and on dark days they shine with surprising brilliance. Though firewood is hard to come by on our side of the lake, I can't bring myself to fall them as long as they appear to be relatively sound. Shorn of twigs and needles they scarcely sway in the heaviest gales while their living colleagues bend and groan in the wind.

Two of them stand in the grassy flat and were dead when I arrived, presumably killed by drowning. Apparently they harbor a sizable population of insects and grubs because the basin's sapsuckers, woodpeckers, and flickers are always noisily at work on them. The two are so riddled with holes they look like targets. Both stand upwind of the cabin, and it is well within their reach though there are several live trees in between.

On stormy nights, I wonder about their brittle tops, decaying trunks and rotted roots, and whether the intervening trees would break their fall. I know that someday they'll come down, and when the gusts are strong at night it seems foolish to let a pair of widowmakers threaten the cabin, but when daylight comes the risk seems small and the threat is forgotten.

The third tree, only ten feet from the cabin but downwind, I unwittingly killed myself. It rises from the center of the only pocket of soil large enough to filter the water from the shower. Late one fall a friend and I excavated a hundred-gallon hole that wrapped around two sides of the tree. In the process we were forced to cut a few roots, and we bruised a good many others. The following spring the bark on the two-foot diameter trunk began to peel and the needles turned yellow, then brown. The tree died that summer and inside of a year the last needles were gone and the barkless trunk was bleached a satiny white.

Just a few feet away a smaller lodgepole grows close beside the cabin. During our first few summers it rubbed against the edge of the roof in every strong wind. The noise inside the cabin was unnerving as the tree ground away a semi-circle of shingles. Now, fifteen years later, the tree has grown thicker and less willowy and only rarely does it bump against the cabin in a storm —thanks largely, of course, to the hole it carved earlier.

Tree growth generally passes unnoticed, but our hammock has provided clearly visible evidence. Years ago when I first hung it between two lodgepoles at the edge of the back porch, I secured it with ropes just long enough to encircle each tree easily. In five years' time both ropes were too short and I was forced to replace them before hanging the hammock that fifth summer. Each tree's circumference had grown six or seven inches in that time.

Before the back porch was built there was a sickly twelve-inch lodgepole growing where the hammock now swings. On the third day of an August blow Kath came in to tell me it was waving much more than the rest, and sawdust was pouring from a small hole in its trunk. I went out to look. The little tree was swaying as though its trunk had turned to rubber. And as it moved, punky bits of yellow decayed wood tumbled from a crack in the dead wood near the ground. The crack opened and closed like something alive and breathing. Inside the trunk something obviously had snapped and the tree was ready to fall, but the way it was waving I didn't dare cut it. It might well have hit the cabin.

Standing on a ladder I tied my strongest rope to the waving trunk about fifteen feet up. The other end I fastened to the largest tree nearby, leaving plenty of slack. If the sick tree fell it would have to break the rope to hit the cabin. But the tree stayed up through two more days of wind, and when the storm was over I falled it away from the cabin. When I examined the trunk I found an inch-thick shell of sound wood surrounding a core of powdered decay. Dozens of fat white grubs had eaten out the tree's heart. I collected them and threw them off the ledge to the trout.

One of the tallest lodgepoles on Upper Granite grows near the water in the grassy flat. On quiet summer evenings I often go canoeing up the lake for an hour before bed, gliding in and out of bays, skirting the islands and rocks. Without a light my eyes soon become accustomed to the dark. I always find my way home sometime around midnight by locating that tall lodgepole silhouetted faintly against the starlit sky and using it as a beacon to guide me back to the harbor.

The forest near the cabin seems to be exclusively lodgepole, but a careful inventory reveals at least a dozen junipers, two mountain hemlock and a single Jeffrey pine. The junipers, except for one misplaced specimen near the outhouse, all grow from seemingly soilless cracks in the windy rock bluff that fronts the lake. So strong and relentless is the wind on this bluff that only one juniper stands upright. The others are no more than gnarled hedges that hug the ground, providing admirable forts and hideouts for my daughter and her friends.

Not a hundred yards to the south, across the channel, lodge-pole are scarce. The forest is solid hemlock, with drooping turquoise branches. On my side of the channel there are only two hemlock, an uncharacteristically twisted pair that grow among the alders in the shadiest part of the swamp. The lone Jeffrey pine, a species that usually seeks shelter and decent soil, grows from the top of the windy granite bluff behind the cove, a site better suited to juniper. At the end of each winter its long needles are snowburned a sickly yellow-brown and the tree seems close to death, but by the end of summer a healthy grey-green color has somehow returned. In the decade and a half we have watched this struggle, the windswept little pine has shown no sign of growth and it has yet to reach a height of six feet.

In our first years at the cabin the monotony of the lodgepole forest induced me to plant other species in hopes of adding variety. Since hemlock grew so gracefully just across the channel I took the boat to Cornell Cove and dug up three trees with relatively undisturbed root systems. They were carefully plant-ed in the finest sites I could find near the cabin: in pockets of rich soil with the best possible combination of drainage, water, shade, and shelter from the wind. They were watered all sum-mer and into the fall, and stoutly staked against the snow. In late October they seemed perfectly healthy, but when the snowpack melted the following spring they were dead.

Thinking I might have transplanted too late, I dug up three more hemlocks before the spring snow was gone, planted them carefully and fed them with vitamin B to minimize shock. One died the first winter, another the second, but the third, though it lost every needle, survived. But five years passed before it fully recovered and put on two inches of powder-blue new growth. Since root damage seemed to be my principal problem I went to a nursery and bought half a dozen assorted conifers that seemed well-suited to the climate. All but one were dead within two years.

In the meantime I transplanted six young aspens from across the lake. I looked forward to the rattle of their apple-green leaves in summer winds and brilliant color in the fall, but none of them survived. In fact most of them were dead by midsummer. My transplanting efforts were not confined to trees. Two hundred yards from the cabin on a dry rocky slope grow luxuriant patches of a jade-green succulent. The clumps I planted near the cabin all died within a month. So did the aromatic sage I brought from a nearby high desert.

My most naive experiment involved the brilliant red asparagus-like snowplant, a saprophyte that lives off decayed organic matter. In the backcountry one day Mike and I found so many of these comparatively scarce plants, all going to seed, that we felt justified in filling a plastic bag with dried flowers. With visions of snowplants everywhere next spring, we planted dozens of seeds in the deepest humus we could find around our cabins. We're still waiting for the first red sprout.

Ten years have passed since I gave up transplanting, and all that survive of the thirty-odd seedlings I tucked in the ground are two healthy hemlocks and one clump of needles on an otherwise dead yellow pine from the nursery. In that same period, as though to mock my efforts, more than a hundred lodgepole seedlings have sprouted around the cabin. Though I have long since bowed to natural selection I still yearn in the fall for the bright yellow aspen that light the dark hemlock forest across the lake. I recently discovered a new source of seedlings, so perhaps next summer I'll try again.

EIGHT

Up on Star Peak

Over the years, especially those spent rebuilding the cabin, I have found it refreshing to go off by myself for a day in the wilds beyond the basin. Before very long massive Star Peak, rising just behind the cabin, became my favorite destination. It is wild and close, and generally I have it to myself. There are no lakes or streams to draw fishermen, and little of the peak is steep enough to interest serious mountaineers. Despite its unpopularity it offers many square miles of lovely varied high-mountain terrain.

In my years of aimless wandering I have come to know a good many of its secrets—hidden springs, forgotten camps, unsuspected hanging valleys, rich gardens, strange formations, corniced cliffs, a lost cabin, caves, quartz veins, deep forests, dramatic weather, and a surprising wildlife population.

Because I always plan to return to the cabin by dark—or soon thereafter—for dinner, I need only to pack a small knapsack with a large lunch, a few survival items, my windbreaker and sweater, and set forth in shorts and boots for the 1500-foot climb to the nearly 9000-foot summit. Along the way I stop in favorite haunts and explore new byways, spending the day enjoying the heights until the setting sun sends me homeward, usually by a different route, comfortably weary and thoroughly refreshed.

The base of the mountain is only a five-minute walk from the cabin. Once I am past the last of the cabins and have crossed the big trail that leads around the lakes, there is just the faint path that follows the buried pipeline climbing to the spring. In a tree-shaded hollow I pause at the two redwood water tanks that function as our reservoir to listen to the gushing water before climbing through brush to cross the old trail, once the route of pack trains headed for the backcountry, but now traveled more by wildlife than humans.

Here in the little flat between aptly named Red Hill and the base of the peak, the Indians who fished and trapped half a century before are supposed to have buried their dead. No one can remember the origin of this legend, but old-timers are said to have found arrowheads and other artifacts in this flat, sheltered spot. Certainly the soft soil would have made digging easy. Kath and I have spent several windy afternoons poking around among suspiciously arranged heaps of stones in hopes of finding further evidence—without success. But still we like to think there are Indians buried in this peaceful place.

Just a few yards away, the rounded summit of Red Hill commands an excellent view not only of both lakes but of the pack trail that circles its base. Ever since she was old enough to reach it on excursions with her friends, Kath has thought of the hill as a playground. She and her friends have built elaborate forts and hideouts, and when they were young they often spent the day playing house, cooking lunch, sliding on snowbanks and spying on unsuspecting hikers below.

Beyond Red Hill the route of the pipeline is rocky, steep, and shadeless, and I think of the men—some of them my friends—who dug arrow-straight trenches through the hot, rusty rock in order to bury the heavy lengths of pipe they carried up from the lakeshore. Their work was so thorough that after a few winters it became almost impossible to see the pipeline's route. A pair of handsome junipers mark an outcropping of dramatic rock: black, white, and strawberry red. When I was gathering rocks for the facing of the fireplace, I walked up after dinner with friends one evening, and each of us carried down the best flat sample he could find, several of which were used above the hearth.

The steep rocky slope ends at the foot of granite cliffs. Fortunately they are breeched by a long slanting ledge which offers the only access to the mountain's upper slopes. A little way up the water-smoothed ramp I stop to listen to a wheeze and gurgle

119

in the brush against the cliff. The first time I heard it, it sounded like some large creature dying, and I approached with trepidation. It turned out that winter drifts had driven the waterpipe (plastic at this point) into a sharp rock, opening a three-inch gash. The rhythmic wheeze and gurgle were produced when the pipe alternately sucked air and spurted water. When Mike repaired the break, the death rattle ceased.

Near the top of the ledge, where it starts to level off, there is a narrow cleft in the sheer granite wall. I climb to its base and sit down on a rock by the battered aluminum cover of the spring. A faucet protrudes from beneath the cover, and when my breathing subsides so I can hear the muffled sound of rushing underground water, I reach into a niche for the ancient cup that has stood there for years, pour myself a drink of the world's finest water and down it in one great quenching gulp. Then I refill the cup, lean back against the cliff and survey the basin spread before me, taking small sips so I can savor the flavor without becoming bloated.

I have sat on this perch and enjoyed this cold water from deep within the mountain in all kinds of weather—in hot dry winds that made me want to stay and sip all day, as well as in rain, hail, snow, and booming thunderstorms in which lightning could be seen striking wildly throughout the basin and the thunder seemed almost continuous, each fresh boom creating strange harmonics with its still echoing predecessors. At times the clouds would descend around the ledge, hiding the basin below.

In one heavy rainstorm that caught me on the ledge, I found admirable and unsuspected shelter a few yards from the spring in a network of caves formed by a jumble of huge granite slabs that had fallen from the cliffs above. For half an hour I lay snug and dry in the warm sand beneath the slab roof while the rain poured down, forming tiny rills in the sand all around me. Tucked away behind the caves is a grassy flat the size of a living room carpet, and it occurred to me the place would make a cozy camp.

A few weeks later, accompanied by friends, I brought the family up on an overnight trip. While the kids gathered firewood and drew water from the spring, we unpacked the beds and cooked the communal dinner. We carried it out to the edge of

the cliff to watch the sunset in the basin below. When the long summer evening gave way to night and the lights came on in the cabins below, the children exchanged Morse code messages by flashlight with their friends below. Then we built up the fire for roast marshmallows and tea before bed. When we left after breakfast the following morning, we cached our grill in a brushy crack, in case we wanted to return. I never pass the cache without checking to make sure it's still there.

Only fifty yards down the cliff below the spring is a genuine cave. I first noticed it while gazing out the window of a lower lake cabin one afternoon. Its black mouth was intriguing and it seemed reasonably accessible from a network of ledges. One day in early July I made my way at last to its shadowy mouth. Dripping water from shaded snowbanks above made a rainlike cur-

121

tain across the entrance. I jumped through the icy curtain to find myself in a shallow humid room with a ceiling of velvety green moss. Luxuriant ferns grew from cracks in the sandy floor. But the caverns and tunnels to the middle of the mountain that I'd imagined did not exist. Despite its black entrance, the cave was only fifteen feet deep.

The ledge on which we camped comes abruptly to an end fifty yards beyond the spring, and we must scramble up a steep game trail through the brush, clutching at rocks and tree roots for support, to reach the mountain's upper slopes in a small hanging valley I call "the park." Floored in white granite sand this gently sloping glacial cirque shelters a parklike grove of pine, fir, and hemlock. Huge decaying logs and massive stumps, from far larger trees than those that remain, show this country enjoyed a considerably wetter climate in the preceding century.

When I first reach the park, usually in May, the only footprints I find in the snow and wet sand are those of the mule deer who have passed through the valley on their way to graze on the sage plain above. Later in the spring I also find tracks of other mammals living high on the mountain: the coyote, snowshoe rabbit, yellow-bellied marmot, and the rare mountain lion that comes to stalk deer. Though the park is open woodland and easily traveled, the wildlife sticks slavishly to the three or four well-worn game trails that cross it.

Near the edge of the cliff one day in early spring, I spotted a pair of large charcoal brown birds in the dead spike top of a pine. Keeping out of sight, I worked my way toward them through the trees. When at last they saw me there was a single loud cry and they leaped in the air, beating huge wings before gliding out over the lip of the valley and into the thermals of rising air. Their color, cry, and size, together with the white on the undersides of their wings, marked them as young golden eagles.

Perhaps fifty feet apart, one bird higher and leading, they soared on flat wings in a long climbing arc that took them off to the west and into the prevailing wind. The sight of those two majestic birds floating away to disappear behind Rainbow Peak made the country seem incomparably wild.

Near the top of the park on the way to the sage plain above, I pass a scattering of charred twigs in the sand near the trunk of a large yellow pine. Years before, caught on the sage plain by a sudden storm, three of us had run down the sandy slope and flung ourselves beneath the pine's convenient umbrella. The wind was cold and we were dressed in shorts, so we built a small fire of handy pine cones and branches and huddled close around it to keep ourselves warm and to keep the fire from blowing away.

For perhaps twenty minutes the storm raged around us, the wind blowing bits of our fire down the valley, yellow bolts of lightning stabbing the darkness of the basin below. Then as quickly as it came the storm disappeared. Before we could put out our fire and move on, steam was rising from the sun-warmed sand.

At the top of the park I can look down the mountain's steep north face a thousand feet into a glacially carved cirque that holds the ruins of a mountain lake turning rapidly to meadow. Wondering what it was like there, I once climbed up from below through brushfields that badly scratched my legs to find a pond of open water ringed by lush marsh teeming with life. Guarded by sheer cliffs above and deep brush below, the little oasis was a wildlife sanctuary well fortified against man's intrusion. I may have been its first visitor in decades.

My favorite route through the park to the sage plain below the summit makes a climbing half-circle to the shoulder of the peak at the top of the cliff above the spring. Here I often stop to sit regally in one of half a dozen thrones and survey the basin below. In this massive but delicately sculpted outcropping dozens, maybe hundreds, of cups, bowls, potholes, and sinks are carved out of the granite where softer stone was easily eroded. Water in little potholes is still fresh and cold a week after a rain—provided it is free of marmot droppings.

If the weather is fine, I settle back in the most comfortable throne to scan the other peaks for climbers, look for deer in the willow thickets of Talking Mountain's avalanche chutes, and watch the changing wind patterns on the surface of the lakes far below. When the wind is heavy or it is cold on the mountain I forego my throne and climb down into the shoulder's largest chamber, big enough for me to stretch out full length on its sandy floor. There I can comfortably bask in the sun or eat my lunch in perfect comfort while the wind whips by only four feet above.

One day I decided to climb straight up from the spring ledge to the thrones by way of a series of crevices and ledges. On the first ledge I found three lumps of pure white quartz, and more on the next ledge. Remembering how my prospector friend Murl had taught me to trace the rock we found in desert washes to its source in the mountain, I decided to search for the lode. No prospector passes up a chance to find a quartz vein, and high-grade gold ore had been found not three miles away.

The higher I went the more quartz I found, and halfway up the cliff I spied above me on the wall a glittering opening in the granite. Scrambling up a crack, I wriggled my way along a narrow ledge on my stomach until I reached the vein, which was hollowed out to a depth of two feet. The entire inner surface was lined with jagged quartz crystals, some of it so rotten it came away in my hand. My position made it awkward to reach in the hollow, but the samples I broke loose showed no sign of free gold. At first I was disappointed, but then I realized Star Peak hardly needed a gold mine.

Behind the thrones and just above the park, a broad shelter-less sage plain, not unlike an English moor, slopes up toward the distant rocks of the summit. An almost continuous wind keeps it treeless, and in a heavy blow I have often been knocked down by sudden slackenings and gusts. Winds of fifty miles an hour are not unusual, and the desolate plain is often snowfree in midwinter, the only bare ground for many miles.

I first thought it strange to find a bleak rolling plain at the top of a mountain rimmed by glaciated cliffs, but then I saw the obvious explanation. The thousand-foot-thick glaciers that dug Granite Basin and surrounded the peak never reached this high. The sage plain and summit comprised a small island that rose above the ocean of ice.

One day on the trail at the foot of the mountain I met the advance party for a group of scientists bent on proving the earth was rapidly entering a new Ice Age. The summer before, much of the snow from a very heavy winter had failed to melt on the shady northeast slopes of the highest mountains. The névé thus formed, they expected to prove, was building into permanent snowfields that would merge to form an ice cap, which in turn would send new glaciers down the canyons.

A large camp was set up and work began. But the scientists had overlooked one critical fact: the winter just previous had been extremely light. By midsummer the last of the new snow was gone and the névé beneath it was beginning to melt. By mid-August it was clear the thesis had failed, and camp was quietly closed. In the long mellow autumn the last of the névé disappeared.

Even after the mystery of the sage plain was explained, I was puzzled for a while by the game trails that led to it. They were heavily traveled coming up through the park, but when they reached the plain they disappeared entirely within several hundred yards. Again, the explanation was simple. The park offered no browse so there was nothing to distract hungry deer from the trail. The sage plain, however, offered excellent browse. Once the deer arrived they spread out to feed at random—and therefore left no discernible trail.

The sage plain appeared featureless at first but over the years I have discovered several landmarks. There is the hidden hollow where I once surprised two grazing fawns, an outcropping of pink quartz, an unexplained cairn in the middle of nowhere that might mark a grave, and the boulder that marks a grave I dug myself. One day in July I was walking up the plain toward the summit with friends while their black labrador puppy bounded ahead, exploring. All at once the dog took off up the slope and pounced on what was evidently an old or sleepy marmot before it could reach the safety of its den. By the time we caught up and pulled the dog off, the animal was badly maimed, and I was forced to kill and bury it.

At the top of the sage plain lies Star Peak's summit, an outcropping of rock carved by water and wind into potholes and hollows like those at the thrones. After walking to the summit across a rolling plain, it is something of a shock to reach the edge of a cliff and look down fifteen hundred feet to Alpaca Lakes in a shady glacial cirque directly below. The largest of the potholes, on the brink of the cliff, is just big enough to hold three people and a very small fire. To escape the noise of fireworks one Fourth of July, three of us decided to carry our beds to the top of Star Peak and spend the night.

It was a warm, still evening by Star Peak standards, with only a faint breeze at the summit. There was just enough room to sit snugly in the pothole, our backs against one wall, while an Indian fire of juniper twigs burned against the other near our feet. From our mountaintop nest we could watch the flares and rockets arc out across the dark water of Piute Lake—miles away and thousands of feet below—in a silence so deep we could only hear the crackle and hiss of the fire.

Alpaca Lakes, though hardly bigger than ponds, boast six or seven cabins and a rustic resort that lie half a mile by trail from the end of the road. One fine July day, after a family shopping trip to the nearby town of Celio, we followed the winding mountain road to its end and walked in to the lakes for lunch on a terrace overlooking the upper lake. The north face of Star Peak rose straight out of the lake and looked unclimbable without a rope, but I was told there was a steep and circuitous route to the summit. I had brought my boots, so when Freda and Kath headed back to the car I climbed over the mountain and down the other side to meet them back at the cabin.

When I reach the summit, I'm usually ready for a drink of cold water or a bottle of lemonade to go with my lunch. Soon after a rain I can find cool water in a shaded summit pothole that hasn't yet been fouled by marmots, but the remains of a cornice on the peak's north rim is a colder and more dependable source. Early in the season I needn't move more than fifty feet from the summit to hold my waterbottle beneath the dripping curled lip of the ice. And if I'm hot enough from climbing I may carefully clamber down beneath the overhanging ice into a blue-tinted snow cave for a shower that cools me very quickly. Often while eating my lunch on the summit I have heard a loud crack and watched tons of overhanging cornice break free and crash down the mountain toward Upper Alpaca, so I never linger in the icy shower!

Later in the year I may have to walk several hundred yards to a shaded semi-permanent snowfield for water. There I am obliged to dig a hole with my hands in the wet sand at its base. A pond of snowmelt soon forms behind my dam, and inside of five minutes it is perfectly clear and can be carefully dipped out with a small paper cup to fill my bottle.

Sitting on the mountaintop, I never cease to marvel at the sharp change in climate where the north and south summit slopes meet. The south-facing sage plain, scourged by sun and wind, gets scant snow in winter and is as parched as a desert the rest of the year. But just over the crest, on the sheltered north slope, the snow piles deep in corniced drifts that last nearly all year, supporting a luxuriant forest of pine, fir, and hemlock. Not far below the summit on this lush wooded slope I make an annual harvest of aromatic pennyroyal. Its crushed leaves add a fresh minty flavor to my lemonade, and all winter long it brings flavor and fragrance to my nightly pot of tea.

Once on top of the summit ridge, with its exhilarating height and marvelous views, I like to stay there as long as I can. Wandering one day on the peak's upper slopes, I discovered a long-forgotten path up its forested western ridge. Though shown on no maps and in places quite faint, this trail gave evidence of being quite old, and apparently at one time it was heavily traveled. I wondered who had built it, and why. It was several years before I discovered the answers. While criss-crossing the western slope searching for clues, I happened one day on a series of faded orange signs nailed twenty feet above the ground on large trees. "Granite Rim Ski Trail," they read. In the days before helicopters and automatic measuring and recording devices, I found out, a water company patrolman, wintering in an upper lake cabin, had skied this trail periodically to measure the depth of the snow pack. I also found out that a century before dairymen, shepherds, and cattlemen had made good use of the lush meadows of the region. The butter, milk, cheese, beef, and mutton produced were transported down the mountain on pack animals and rafted across Granite Lakes to the immigrant trail that crossed Granite Summit. The hungry pioneers, having wearily dragged their possessions to the crest of the range, willingly paid a stiff price for fresh dairy products and meat. And they were just as happy to buy fresh mountain grasses, cut and baled in a meadow at the foot of Star Peak, for their starving, over-worked oxen.

The old path up Star Peak's long west ridge passes through some of the region's thickest forest. Deep quiet forest, with its soft green light and the presence of gigantic living things, is relatively rare in this high region of bare rock, wind and brilliant light. So I increasingly found myself leaving the trail to wander among the great trunks in the cool, shady, aromatic air to escape the wind and hard light.

It was on one of these aimless forest traverses, crossing a rocky slope high on the peak that I suddenly heard the sound of running water. To my astonishment I discovered a small but vigorous stream—something I'd been sure did not exist on the mountain—tumbling down a dry slope and into a thicket of willow. When I knelt for a drink I found the water surprisingly cold, suggesting it came from a nearby spring. I would have climbed up to look, but it was late in the day, I was miles from the cabin, and a cold wind had turned the day chilly.

Two or three nights later I was visiting my friend Mike in his family's old cabin a hundred yards up the lake, when he made some reference to the shepherd who, half a century before, had grazed a flock of sheep each summer on the sage plain. Mike knew the shepherd had built a cabin somewhere high on the mountain because his grandmother had once taken him to see its remains. That had been fifteen years before and, though Mike had spent many summers in the basin and knew the country well, he had never been able to find the cabin again. He thought it sat quite high, and he remembered there were trees, but he couldn't remember any landmarks.

It occurred to me, as Mike talked, that if the shepherd had built a cabin it must have been close to a dependable source of water. And if his flock grazed the sage plain close beneath the summit, he would surely want his camp as high as he could get it. Since the stream I had found was by far the highest running water on the peak, there was a good chance its source lay close to the shepherd's lost cabin. The thought was exciting and we decided to go hunting the following day.

Approaching as we did from the opposite direction, the stream proved hard to find—until we ran into a thicket of willow. Willow on a south-facing slope means surface water, so we climbed along its margin, and gradually the country began to look familiar. At the top of the thicket we heard the gurgling of water, and there was the little stream, with my footprints still visible in the soft earth beside it. But what excited us even more was a pair of weathered stumps half buried in the brush just a few yards away. Those trees, we were certain, had been felled with an axe! Following the stream we hurried uphill, passing several more stumps, until we entered open forest.

A few yards farther on we reached a little clearing, in the center of which we saw the spring. Water bubbled from the ground to fill a small pool that was formed by the ruin of a small rock dam. Nearby in the weeds we found a battered tin cup. The cabin must be close. We set off from the spring in opposite directions, and only fifty feet away, where the woods gave way to meadow, I came upon the ruin of the cabin. I gave a shout and Mike came to join me.

The cabin consisted of a single room, just ten feet by twelve, built of notched lodgepole logs small enough to be lifted in place by one man. The sagging walls now stood only four logs high, the downhill wall was virtually gone, and a layer of rotting poles on the cabin's dirt floor was all that remained of the fallen-in roof. We made up a bottle of cold lemonade at the spring, discovering in the process the overgrown path the shepherd had used, then returned to the shelter of the cabin for lunch, our backs against the sunny north wall.

Before us the grassy slope dropped away steeply and we looked out across the basin to a succession of little cirques, each with a stream cascading from the mouth, between Talking Mountain and the bare granite cliffs of Rainbow Peak. This was the view the shepherd woke to each morning. What sort of man had he been, I wondered. Did he like the life or simply endure it? Where had he come from and what made him stop coming? Finishing our lunch we continued exploring, searching for clues about the shepherd's life.

Behind the cabin, beneath a layer of pine needles, Mike found a dump of tin cans, but it seemed awfully small for a man who spent at least a dozen summers on the mountain. He might have been too poor to buy his food in cans, but more likely he'd been unable to leave his flock to make the long trip on foot for store-bought provisions. Like many of his kind he had probably

129

lived largely on mutton. Of course the mountain could provide a good deal of food. Miners' lettuce grew by the spring, with a thicket of wild gooseberries just below. He had probably known where to dig wild onions, and the pennyroyal would have kept him in tea. Grouse and porcupine are easy to kill, and he could have trapped rabbits and shot an occasional deer. He might have eaten quite well, we had to conclude, even if he'd brought only sugar, salt and flour.

The cabin showed no sign of a fireplace or stove, which perplexed us at first, but we soon found the shepherd's kitchen fifty feet away. Two enormous windthrown trees formed a v-shaped enclosure well-sheltered from the wind. In the middle, a good-sized fireplace had been carefully constructed of small rocks. Before it a short section of log made a seat, and from the silted over ash heap grew a clump of sage. Despite the many fires that fireplace must have seen, there wasn't a trace of soot on the rock. Over the years the wind, sun, rain and melting snow had completely erased the greasy stain of black smoke, a process that takes more than thirty years. Mike thought the shepherd had last brought his flock in the early nineteen-twenties. If his camp had been used in the last forty years, there had certainly been no fire in that fireplace.

Since that day I have visited the shepherd's cabin often. One July day, friends and I eating lunch there were startled by the sudden furious yelping of a coyote. When the sound continued we imagined the animal must somehow be trapped, and we hurried up the slope toward the noise. We spotted the tawny animal standing in a clearing I didn't remember. Slowly we moved closer in full view of the coyote, but it continued to yelp and made no effort to move.

I was sure it must be badly hurt, but when we approached to within fifty feet, it reluctantly walked off through the trees, occasionally glancing back over its shoulder. When it was gone, we moved into the clearing to inspect the spot where it had stood. There lay an empty, well-rusted sardine can half filled with sand, probably left behind by firefighters. I saw others nearby and realized the clearing must have been made by lightning fire decades before. But we found no clue to what prompted the strange behavior of that howling coyote.

Musing one night about the mountain and its secrets, I found myself wondering where the water from the shepherd's spring went. By August all the streams that reached Upper Granite were dry, while the spring, high above, flowed as strongly as ever. I could have started at the spring and worked my way down, but that would have been too easy. So, starting at the trail that paralleled the lakeshore, I made my way up one stream-bed after another.

Climbing my third stream, half a mile above the lake, I found that some time in the past a crude dam had been built and an aqueduct dug to reroute the stream down an alternate water-course, leading toward a cabin on the shore. The water system had failed when the stubborn stream, refusing to be rechan-neled, had washed out the dam and reverted to its original course. Over the years the canal had silted in, and only its strange configuration led me to discover what it had been and why.

Continuing up the stream I came into a lovely little campsite hidden away in a pocket of forest. A small caved-in fireplace with a rusty wire grate was almost buried in many years' accumula-tion of pine needles.

The campsite obviously had been forgotten by its builders. Thirty feet away a small waterfall dropped into a foaming pool, and I made up some lemonade in my waterbottle and returned to the camp to sit back against a tree and eat my lunch. The steady splash of the waterfall made a pleasant background for the quiet chirping of birds in the trees.

This out-of-the-way camp, with its view across the basin, seemed ideal for a family excursion, so I set about getting it ready. I quickly cleaned out and rebuilt the old fireplace, dis-mantled a useless rock windbreak, collected the scattered fire-wood and pinecones by the fireplace, and fluffed up the matted pine needles in the best bedsites. When I left the little camp it was ready for our overnight visit two weeks later.

Before long the stream disappeared in a waist-high brushfield of bluish buckthorn. At a glance it looked impassable for a traveler in shorts, but it seemed highly likely the deer knew a way to get through. Skirting the brush, inspecting its margin closely, I soon found the narrow opening I sought. The game trail I found was faint and indirect, often turning sharply for no apparent reason, but it took me through the thorn-studded thicket with hardly a scratch.

Once back in the timber, I climbed past a series of waterfalls and small pools. Then the stream forked and I had to make a choice. Though there was brush in that direction, I chose the branch that led steeply toward the sage plain. Climbing mostly on game trails I made my way upward, until I topped a rise and could see another large brush field ahead. But this one looked different. Instead of the blue-white of buckthorn, I saw the glazed red-tipped yellow that meant willow. It proved to be the thicket that spread out beneath the spring, and inside of fifteen minutes I was comfortably seated against the cabin's back wall, happily gulping down cold lemonade. Now I knew how the water from the spring reached the lake. I had also discovered why the stream below went dry when the last snow was melted: the willow thicket drank every drop the spring produced.

Another afternoon, with three hiking companions, I was sitting eating lunch on the mountain's summit, watching storm clouds gather, when a pair of lightning bolts struck nearby. Grabbing our belongings we climbed down from the peak and set out on the run down the sage plain. By the time we reached the sheltering forest rain was falling. Moments later it was pouring and we flattened ourselves against the trunk of the nearest tree. We seemed certain of a soaking until Meg spotted what looked like a hollow log, ran to it, and disappeared inside.

When her head reappeared and she called that there was room for all four of us, we dashed through the rain to dive beneath the log. Half a century before a lightning fire had felled the huge tree and hollowed out its center. In time the soot had weathered away and the weight of the snow had split the log and partially collapsed it, producing a low but admirable roof. We lay tightly packed but comfortable on the dry grass beneath while the rain beat down furiously above. Thunder echoed across the basin and even from our cave we could see the flash of lightning.

Three times the lightning struck so close that flash and crack were almost simultaneous. The last strike brought the sharp smell of woodsmoke, but there was nothing to be seen. For most of an hour we sang, told stories, and listened to the drumming of the rain on our roof. Then the drumming died away and was replaced by the quiet dripping of the trees. We crawled out and hurried down the mountain through the soaking grass and brush. The sky was still dark, the air had turned cold, and evening was approaching. The trail, when we reached it, was a series of puddles which we splashed through with boots already wet from our descent.

That night the sky cleared and hot air from the west came over the ridge to warm the basin. I launched the canoe and paddled up the lake in the dark. Behind an island near the head of the lake I met my friends, who had also been drawn out by the balmy night—and the news of a fire on the ridge. They pointed to the skyline and handed me a pair of binoculars. High on the the mountain where we had waited out the storm in our fire-hollowed log, an isolated juniper was burning like a torch. It was still flaming brightly when we headed for our beds an hour later.

One might reasonably suppose that after fifteen years, I should begin to lose interest in exploring Star Peak, but I haven't. The better I come to know it, the better I like it. The mountain, by now, is an old and trusted friend who never fails to provide the peace and refreshment I seek.

NINE

Mountain Weather

Mountain weather, with its sudden, dramatic changes, has always intrigued me. And for richness and variety it would be hard to surpass the Granite Basin weather. We have snow, wind, hail, avalanche, flood, lightning, waterspouts, dust-devils, mists, heat waves, fog, tropical storms, every kind of cloud, and smoke from forest fires. The lakes provide us with annual freezeups, breakups, and temperature inversions, and when the wind blows a gale we get whitecaps and rollers, spume that blows a hundred feet in the air, and breakers that rip boats from their moorings to sink or hurl them ashore. When the wind is really blowing even the biggest boats in the basin dare not set forth, and lakers are forced to put on their packs to hike in and out for supplies.

Isolated as we are from automobiles, electricity, and phones, weather and season determine our ability to travel to and from the cabin. They thus affect our safety as well as our comfort.

Granite Basin weather is as erratic and unpredictable as it is dramatic. "Average" years are almost unknown. For instance, in an "average" year the ice should go out the last week in May. That's what we plan on, but it never seems to happen. I have seen the lakes clear the first week in May, and I have seen the ice last until July. One October we had forty-two inches of snow in three weeks, but the same month the year before was so warm we spent half of each day swimming and sunning on the white sandy beach in Cornell Cove.

Granite Basin has a well-deserved reputation for wind. The

wind is not incessant, but a day without a breeze is unusual. As cabin sites go, ours is unusually windy, lying as it does at the downwind end of the lake. The evidence has been etched in the pines along the shore. Wind-driven ice crystals shear off new buds every winter, so no branches grow on the trees' windward sides.

Granite Basin can also be cold. The lakes are frozen over for roughly half the year, and snow often falls in the warmest months of summer if protracted storms chill the basin. Annual snowfall sometimes reaches forty feet, and wind-piled drifts twenty feet in depth are not unusual.

But the basin, though never uncomfortably hot, is pleasantly warm for most of the summer. Getting dressed in the morning means putting on a bathing suit, and often in August the nights are too warm to sleep under more than a sheet. Valley air from west of the mountains does a remarkable job of warming the lakes. By the Fourth of July lakewater that was frozen a month before may have reached a swimable sixty-five degrees. Most years the thermometer under our pier reaches seventy, with an all time high of seventy-four.

Granite Basin has a habit of generating its own weather, and many of its most dramatic storms are purely local. In fact the average snowfall one mile south of the basin is only half of what buries Granite Lakes! More than once I've left the basin after three days of storm to find unbroken fair weather only ten miles away.

The weather even varies within the basin. After a morning of rain has kept us in the cabin, I have boated to the Chalet less than two miles away to find the ground perfectly dry.

It isn't just by chance that the Granite Basin weather machine generates wind and snow in such quantity. The basin lies just to the east and not far below the crest of the region's highest mountain range, which intercepts moisture-laden winds approaching from the ocean. Winds passing over a mountain range are markedly compressed, which causes them to accelerate. They are also cooled quickly as they rise to climb over the mountain barrier.

Because Granite Basin runs basically east-west, the prevailing west winds find it the path of least resistance—a ready-made wind tunnel. As the winds descend into the funnel-shaped basin they become further concentrated and wind speed increases. Moisture is easily condensed out of these mountain-cooled winds, bringing rain, hail, and snow to the basin.

The prevailing west wind, flowing virtually unbroken from the Pacific, is the principal force that drives the weather machine, but it has some help. The coastal valley to the west, across which it flows, is lower and warmer than the high inland basin that lies to the east. The temperature differential keeps the air flowing briskly from west to east in a vain attempt to equalize temperature and pressure.

Besides cooling the air, the basin's altitude also affects its density and composition. At a mile and a half above sea level the air is significantly thinner and cleaner, and its oxygen content has dropped about twenty-five percent. Most people, on arriving, are short of breath and inclined to be lethargic for a day or two. A few get headaches and find it difficult to sleep.

Thinner air is comparatively transparent and permits a greater flow of heat radiation—in both directions, changing temperature rapidly. When the day is still one can freeze in the shade or burn in the sun. Untanned skin can suffer severe sunburn in less than thirty minutes because of the unimpeded passage of burning violet and ultraviolet rays through the thin air. The body takes several days to acclimatize to Granite's altitude, but the skin never does. Even the deepest tan is insufficient protection from the burning rays of high-altitude sunlight.

When the sun goes down the dry air quickly turns cold because it cannot hold moisture, and therefore heat. It is fortunate that the basin's persistent breeze—unless there is a storm —characteristically also dies at sunset, largely offsetting the drop in air temperature. Despite the altitude and dryness, midsummer nights are often surprisingly warm. Superheated air from the valley to the west, even after climbing over 9000-foot mountains, is often still warm when it reaches Granite. Starting at as much as a hundred degrees, it can afford to lose thirty and still bring seventy-degree nightime warmth to the basin.

Moist air rising to climb over Talking Mountain, just across the channel, creates a steady stream of cloud that literally materializes out of thick air above the peak. This blowing stream of

condensing cloud, once it passes the crest and enters the drier air beyond, evaporates completely before it has sailed half a mile. When conditions are right, Talking Mountain generates this sort of cloud all day long, like a boiling teakettle, but when the wind dies at dusk the sky is perfectly clear.

After dinner one evening in late April I went for a moonlight walk on the still-frozen lake. Deep snow covered the basin and the temperature was well below freezing. The weather and season seemed perfectly normal, and I shivered as I undressed to climb into my down sleeping bag in the loft. Sometime after midnight a burning sensation awoke me. I was sweating profusely and my bag was soaked. A wind had come up and it was actually hot in the room. I climbed out of the sticky bag and stepped out on the windy porch, naked. A chinook had blown

137

into the basin while I slept and the temperature had risen some forty degrees!

I stood for awhile on the porch in the soft wind, enjoying the night. Except for the snow it might have been August. Had I examined closely I could probably have seen the snow level dropping, for the chinook is one of the driest of winds. Its remarkable ability to evaporate snow has earned it the nickname "snow-eater," and its deeds in snow country are legendary. After turning the down bag inside out to dry, I went back to bed under summer blankets. When I awoke the next morning it was like a summer day and the stream beneath the house was running like a river. But by noon the chinook had entirely disappeared. Clouds began to gather and winter returned.

Equally dramatic was an autumn storm enjoyed by my geologist friend Skip. The lake was down to winter level when he made his way up the basin in the little fiberglass boat we share in the fall. The water was so calm and his lower lake harbor so sheltered from wind that he merely beached the boat in the sand beneath his pier, not bothering to tie it. Soon after dark the wind began to blow and shortly thereafter it started to rain. Rainstorms in the basin are usually soon over, but this one grew heavier by the hour. All night it rained hard and the wind seemed to blow from every direction.

It was still raining hard the following morning when Skip looked down at his harbor. Lower Granite had risen several feet in the night and the boat had disappeared. He ran to a nearby promontory and studied the storm-lashed lake through binoculars. Finally he spotted the little boat bobbing near the willow-lined shore a mile away on the far side of the channel. He set off on the run down the shore, splashing through the thigh-deep torrent of the channel, and finally reached the willows. The half-filled boat was wallowing sluggishly, the nearly submerged motor dragging it down.

Already soaked, Skip waded out among the willows until he could just reach the boat with an oar. He finally coaxed it close enough to grab the bow line and drag it to shore. The storm ended before sunset and the next day there wasn't a cloud in the sky. But in the space of less than twenty-four hours so much rain had fallen in the basin that Upper Granite had risen more than four feet—from low water to flood! The channel, which had been dry when Skip arrived, was still navigable to boats a week later. By that time the upper lake level had subsided, but windrows of pine needles covering my pier showed how high the flood had reached.

Another year, spring turned to summer with startling suddenness in the middle of June. Every day for two weeks the weather had been windy and snow had fallen in the afternoon. Late in the day I sat close to the stove, heavily dressed, watching as gusts of wind come rushing down the lake beneath the dense clouds that earlier had brought snow. Out among the islands they first became visible as distant dark patches on the lake's grey surface. Like the shadows of clouds they swiftly moved toward me, gathering speed as they crossed the reef, passed the pier and drove into the cove. They leaped the bank, flattening the grass, and I braced myself for the sudden roar that came when a gust reached the trees. An instant later the wind struck the cabin with a jolt that made it creak, and the kitchen window through which I watched bent alarmingly inward, distorting my view as it flexed. The stovepipe hummed and the guy wires sang, then the gust was gone, and in the lull before the next it was almost still.

That night it was cold but the sky was clear, and the morning dawned bright and perfectly still. There wasn't a cloud or even a breeze, and by late afternoon it was genuinely hot. Yesterday's parka and boots were set aside, and I was comfortably warm in swim trunks and bare feet. In fact the pier got so hot I had to dip my feet periodically in the lake to keep them from burning. The evening was so balmy I was still canoeing beneath the full moon at midnight. All of a sudden it was summer.

The southern slope of Granite Basin is nearly vertical in spots, so it's not surprising, given the heavy snowfall, that the avalanche hazard in spring is often great when weather conditions make for unstable snow. Since 1948 no less than fourteen cabins have been destroyed by falling ice and snow or the terrible winds that accompany them.

On Talking Mountain and its ridges unstable conditions develop when one of two things happen. Either a warm storm dumps wet heavy snow that builds up until its weight is too great to cling to the precipitous slope, or a thaw melts the surface, then the freezing that follows turns the surface to slick ice. Subsequent snowfall sticks poorly to the ice, and a comparatively small buildup is likely to slide.

A third familiar cause is the late spring increase in weight as snowmelt water saturates the snowpack. Owners can't be sure their cabins have survived another winter until the cornices above them are substantially melted. The potential danger can last into July.

The spring avalanche hazard is much like the danger of spring flood, in fact the two are sometimes related. The same tropical rainstorms that melt the snow in midwinter are responsible for the periodic floods that lift the upper lake ice and destroy every pier in its grip. The same thing happens in spring when warm wind or rain so accelerates the melting of the snowpack that the channel can't accommodate all the snowmelt that pours into the upper lake.

At the cabin spring floods usually mean that the grassy flat and the pier's outer span are under water for a day or two in early June and the channel overflows its banks for a week until a cool spell slows down the melt.

Though largely independent of the weather, forest fire danger belongs in a class with avalanche and flood. Kath and I had driven halfway to the cabin from the city one August morning when the radio reported our customary route was closed by a rampaging forest fire that had jumped the highway, burned several thousand acres in a matter of hours and was still out of control. The mountain communities closest to Granite Basin had already been evacuated. Although the highway from which the basin road branched was closed, we decided to take a chance on getting in from the other side of the mountain.

After a long, roundabout trip we reached the highway blockade, and the patrolman let us through when I convinced him we owned a place at Granite. The basin was largely deserted and a thick pall of smoke hung over the lakes. Upper lake neighbors assured us the fire was not expected to climb into the basin— unless the wind grew strong. Later that afternoon the smoke was so dense that visibility shrank to a few hundred feet. The nearest

140

upper lake islands were lost in the gloom. Without the small breeze we would have been forced to evacuate.

That night Mike climbed the ridge to observe and reported the flames were some distance away. The following day visibility improved. The breeze continued mild and the basin remained safe, but the fire was out of control for a week. The transcontinental highway stayed closed for nine days, and it was nearly two weeks before the last spark was out and the sky in the basin was smokefree and blue.

Since storms are at their worst on the shelterless lakes, boating adventures are unavoidable. One nasty afternoon in June, Rafferty and I were stuck at the Chalet with a boatload of lumber when fog lowered to the water and it started to snow. We sat before the fire and waited for clearing weather, but several hours later the snow was still falling. Since the fog refused to lift and darkness was approaching, I decided to try to find my way up the lake. It was either that or leave the boat and walk.

Steering with one hand and steadying the stack of sixteen-foot planks with the other, I pulled out of the harbor and aimed the boat in the direction of the channel. But once the docks were behind us the mists closed in around us, and there was no way to tell where we were headed. We plowed through the fog and falling snow, and just when I judged we should sight shore directly ahead, it mysteriously appeared on our right: ghostly trees in the mist and wet rocks.

It looked totally unfamiliar and the rocks in the water were menacing enough to make me veer sharply to the left, away from shore. A minute or two passed and then another strange section of shore appeared on my right. I hadn't the slightest idea where I was but again I veered left into the mists. Then a boat took shape in the fog nearby, but before I was close enough to ask where we were it fell in behind me and started to follow.

Twice more I sighted land—always on my right—and veered away. Gradually I came to realize I had been zigzagging up the lake's eastern shore. My estimate of time, direction and distance had become temporarily confused, but now I had to be approaching the upper end of the lake. Straining to see through the swirling fog I finally spotted a familiar stretch of shore. A moment later the pier beside the channel took shape, and there was someone on it waving. It was Freda. Worried by my absence she had walked to the lower lake to watch and wait.

Though summer has usually arrived by July, it can still lapse into winter, especially in the wilderness behind Granite Basin. Spring was stormy and cold the year Kath was five, but after two weeks of warm weather in the basin it looked like summer and we decided to take a short walk to a backcountry lake for a picnic lunch. I also looked forward to casting flies for brook trout. After an early breakfast we packed everything except the camera and my fly rod in Rafferty's pack, took the boat to the landing at the head of the lake, and started up the trail. The morning was cloudless and still, the air beginning to warm.

When we turned off onto the faint path that led to Star Lake I was pleased to find the damp sand free of footprints. We would be the first visitors of the year. As we entered deeper forest, snowbanks began to appear, and before we reached the pass that led out of the basin, the trail had disappeared beneath a snow-pack three to five feet deep. That was slightly disconcerting but the family seemed content, the weather was warm, and there was only half a mile to go. Forgetting he wore a pack, Rafferty tried to squeeze between two trees and got stuck, and Kath fell down a few times in the snow, but we reached Star without difficulty, sliding down a snow slope to the shore.

There was open ground in a campsite by the lake, and after unpacking Raff and turning him loose to romp, I quickly set up my rod. Trout were rising in a nearby cove and I landed a pair before stopping to build a fire for lunch. We cooked hotdogs to go with lemonade and hardboiled eggs, and I was thinking of more fish when a shadow fell over camp.

The sky was swiftly filling with cloud. We should have made a run for it then, I suppose, but I hoped for more trout and a storm seemed unlikely. It was too nice a day.

I gathered extra wood, built the fire high and went fishing. The sky rapidly grew dark and when it started to rain I hurried back to camp and built a roof of damp bark above the fire. Fifteen feet away Freda, Kath and Raff were anxiously huddled in a hollow between two trees. When the rain grew stronger I built a rock wall behind them for added protection. By the time

I was finished it was snowing. After piling all our firewood against one of the trees, I uncovered the fire and dragged the flaming logs to the mouth of the hollow where I quickly built a blaze that kept us warm. Fortunately neither of the ladies had gotten wet and I soon managed to dry my wet shirt above the flames.

For probably two hours, snuggled tightly together, we watched the falling snow, fed the fire and waited. I repeatedly assured the family the storm wouldn't last and we were wiser to stay dry and try to wait it out than set forth and get wet. There was plenty of time to get home before dark since we were less than a mile and a half from the boat. When the snow turned to rain and finally stopped, Freda was determined to get started. I told her we should stay another thirty minutes, but she was too cold to wait any longer. We loaded Raff's pack and I picked up Katherine and kicked a line of steps up the snowbank that led toward the pass.

The snow had turned mushy, trees dripped water down our necks and we sloshed through the puddles that filled every depression. Before we reached the pass it started raining again, and this time we got wet, but activity kept us from getting chilled. We slipped and slithered through the pass and by the time we started down to the lake the rain had stopped. The sun was out when we reached the main trail, and before we got home there wasn't a cloud in the sky!

One of the most memorable and dramatic of Granite storms swept in later that same summer, in early August. I was lying in the sun after lunch talking with a neighbor at his lower lake harbor. We were idly watching the buildup of thunderheads off to the east when thunder cracked behind us. We turned to see a mass of black cloud advancing down the basin, its menacing underside only a hundred feet above the basin floor. The air was deathly still and had an ominous quality difficult to describe. My neighbors' kids and Kath, dressed like us in bathing suits, were playing somewhere in kayaks in the upper lake. Lightning struck as we watched, the yellow bolt brilliant against the black of the cloud.

I jumped in my boat and cranked up the engine, but before I reached the channel there was a flash and a simultaneous explosion beside me. From the throttle in my hand came an electrical jolt that knocked me off the seat. For a moment—body tingling, ears ringing—I thought I must have been struck, then I managed to recover and guide the boat into the channel. There was an acrid, pungent smell of ozone in the air and I could feel the hair standing out on my body.

I was barely out of the channel and into Upper Granite when the dead calm was broken by a sudden wild wind that blew from every direction. Momentarily expecting another bolt of lightning, I rocketed around the point into Cornell Cove, and seeing no kayaks sped off across the lake. The rolling mass of black cloud now covered the sky, and it was fast getting dark. The sudden wind stopped and heavy rain began to fall. The lake was entirely deserted. Keeping close enough to land to see through the gloom, I followed the deeply scalloped lakeshore toward the west until at last, with relief, I spotted Kath's green kayak pulled up on shore in a cove beneath an old log cabin belonging to friends.

I moored my boat to a pier and hurried up the path through the heavy rain. Kath and her friends, comfortable and dry, were sitting in their swim suits before the massive fireplace, eating fresh popped corn and roasting marshmallows. They scarcely looked up when I entered. The rain, unbelievably, grew stronger and stronger, and we were forced to shout to make ourselves heard above the roar on the roof. The air outside turned cold and we built the fire higher. The rain turned to hail with undiminished intensity, and needles, twigs, and cones were stripped from the trees by the storm.

From a window by the fire, through a rift in the cloud, I glimpsed Rainbow Peak at the head of the basin. Every crevice in its bare granite face was a vertical white water cataract. Thunder continued to boom in the basin, echoing and reechoing between the granite walls, creating a confusion of deep, hollow booming. From time to time a lightning flash would light up the gloom and I would count off the seconds to see how close it was striking. Gradually the storm moved eastward down the basin and the rain began to lessen, then stopped. As we prepared to leave I realized my hand was still tingling from the lightning shock an hour before!

About an hour after dinner the stillness was broken by thunder in the west. It grew gradually louder like advancing artillery, and the flickering light behind the mountains grew brighter. Then the storm topped the ridge and slipped back into the basin, bringing with it a lightning display unequaled in my experience. For more than two hours the sky was almost continuously lighted by a brilliant spiderweb of light. Strikes averaged less than a second apart, and the light in the loft, where we sat by the windows, was sufficiently bright and continuous to read by! Most of the strikes were a mile or more away, according to my timing, but two deafening bolts must have struck within a few hundred yards of the cabin. It was amazing, with all those strikes, that no cabins were hit, and only the heavy rain prevented lightning fires. Except for debris that covered the ground and floated on the lake, there was scarcely a sign the following day that a storm had lashed the basin, although the odor of ozone remained until the afternoon breeze dispersed it.

Thunderstorms, no matter how fierce, come so seldom in the summer and bring so much drama that most of us view them as splendid entertainment. The same cannot be said of the dreaded and more familiar "blows." When the wind has been blowing hard much of the day, tension begins to mount as the critical hour of sunset approaches. If the wind swiftly dies, as it usually does at dusk, the night will be still and the following day will dawn fair. But if the wind fails to die it means a blow has begun, and there is no way to know when it will stop.

The average blow lasts two or three days, but all of us remember times when the wind has blown for a week or more. The longest I have suffered is eleven days, by which time the basin was practically empty. My journal records what a long blow was like one otherwise mild July.

The first night of wind it is especially hard to sleep. Nights in the basin are usually so still that the incessant sound is unsettling. The old anxiety returns about the thirteen trees, two of them dead, that strain in the wind just a few yards upwind of our bed in the loft. Nothing is easier when the wind blows hard than to lie awake and wait for the grandaddy gust that will uproot a tree and hurl it against the wall at our heads.

Somewhere a loose board occasionally bangs, the window

screens rattle, and the roof makes a vibrating hum. The trees seem to groan as they rub against one another; flying needles brush the window and wind-driven pine cones hit the cabin with a crack. In the moments between gusts we hear the lapping waves splashing at the back of the cove, and I can't help but wonder about the boats and the pier though I checked them by flashlight just before I came to bed.

Once a blow has begun, my first concern is the harbor. I check all the lines and bring in the kayaks that customarily sit on the end of the dock. They are turned upside down on top of the mattress and wedged beneath the massive picnic table. Too often they've blown away and I've been unable to hunt them down for days. Hardly a blow passes without boats being sunk, and my own have gone to the bottom more than once. When the harbor is secure, I check the lumber pile. Once a full sheet of plywood sitting on the pier was picked up and blown against the cabin. If the tent is up I check the poles and lines, and the outhouse door must always be latched. In a blow one year it was literally torn from its hinges.

On the second day of this particular blow the weather is mild and there is no temperature drop in the air of the lake, and I spend the morning sawing and chopping wood. Since there is time enough in the evening for reading, watching the lake occupies the afternoon. During a blow the patterns of whitecaps and seething froth are always changing. For a while the lake is an orderly succession of big green rollers, much like ocean swells, that methodically break across the pier and the breakwater at the back of the cove. Then the wind changes to shear the top off waves, producing a mist of flying spume that billows a hundred feet above the water.

Late in the day we hear a boat nearby and hurry to a window in the loft. It comes slowly up the channel, accelerating now and then to lift the bow above the oncoming waves. The boatman, wearing slicker, wool cap, and mittens, stands at the wheel, feet braced, hanging onto the deck with his free hand, trying to duck the lashing spray. Behind him, crouched low in the cockpit, an unlucky passenger, dressed in light clothing, tries to keep himself wrapped in a poncho while holding on tight. The driver gives his boat all the speed he dares and soon disappears in the blowing spume. Five minutes later the boat reappears running with the waves, headed for the channel, carrying a dozen backpackers huddled together beneath a huge tarp. As the boat cuts through the rollers geysers of spray shoot fifty feet in the air.

On the second night at sunset, the critical hour, we listen and watch for any drop in the wind, but it's blowing harder than ever. For the tenth time that day I tap the barometer. After holding steady through the first twenty-four hours, it has been slowly dropping since noon. The six o'clock weather forecast on the portable radio is equally depressing. After dinner we move out of the kitchen and into the parlor, away from the worst of the noise and heavy drafts. It is cool enough tonight for a fire in the fireplace. With the curtains drawn it is cheerful and snug and we tune out the wind as we read and talk and drink tea, staying up until we're sure we can sleep through the noise.

The third day dawns worse, after a fitful sleep, and there seems little reason to get out of bed into the chilly draft that billows the curtains in the loft. The lake is a maelstrom; I can hardly see across it, and I know that no boats will put out today. The risk of destruction is too great. The sky is a dazzling blue, the sun burns brightly, but the cabin trembles and shudders beneath the onslaught and I wonder if the wind in the streambed beneath it could lift it free of its foundations. Not two hundred yards away a much smaller cabin was blown over onto its roof some years before. And the cabin next door to it, as big as ours, was lifted and shoved two feet off its foundations.

The wind is blowing too hard to use the unsheltered kitchen door and I slide the bolt closed and notify the family before leaving by the back door to check the harbor. Wind beneath the mattress has lifted the two kayaks and turned them sideways, but the massive table has kept them from flying away. I wedge the boats tightly and lash their bows to the tree in the deck. The dock thermometer has disappeared and Kath's swing has blown ten feet into a tree behind it, but the boats are safely bobbing on their moorings and there isn't enough water in the hulls to bail. Rollers are breaking across the pier's outer span and it trembles and sways, but there isn't a thing I can do—except stay off it— after quickly checking the lines.

After breakfast I check the cabin. A screen has been torn off a window in the night, but that's the only damage. From across the lake comes an intermittent ringing, like a Chinese gong, and I take binoculars to the loft to have a look. At a cabin on the point a fifty-five gallon drum, escaped from someone's raft, is banging on the rocks. I also discover the cabin's motorboat has sunk and its sailboat has broken free and been driven onto the rocks. There is nothing to be done, but I make a mental note to notify someone at the Chalet who will phone the absent owners.

We need a few supplies and there is no better way to spend a windy day than making the five mile roundtrip walk to the Chalet. Freda holes up by the fire with a book and Kath leaves to play with her friends, the twins, at a nearby cabin. It feels good to get out on the trail with a light pack and I am quickly reminded, as I walk, that ours is one of the windiest locations in the basin. On the trail I meet several friends on similar missions. One has a newspaper whose forecast fails to hint at wind. The other has been out of the basin to shop. Ten miles away, she says, the weather is quiet and warm, without a sign of wind! At the Chalet a boatman tells me one of the taxis hit a rock in the channel early that morning, destroying the engine's lower unit. He knows of two sunken boats besides the one I report, and three more in the harbor that were rescued just in time.

That night the wind produces a siren-like shriek in the loft door keyhole, and we decide to spend the night in the comparative quiet of the parlor. On the morning of the fourth day my shower is cold, and I discover the wind has blown out the water heater's pilot. Though the sun still shines in a cloudless sky the air outside is cooler, and the spray off the lake, when I go to check the boats, is decidedly cold. In early afternoon a metallic banging on the roof reveals that some of the aluminum sheathing has come loose, and I promptly climb up to nail it down before the wind can get beneath it and rip off the roof. When I am through, Kath brings me a hinged outhouse shutter she found in the path.

After lunch I sit in the sunny loft in a swim suit, alternately reading and watching the storm-lashed lake. A seagull struggling against the wind beats its wings hard but makes little headway. At times he is standing still. Then he gives up and turns to rocket downwind out of sight. By the afternoon of the fourth day everyone remaining in the basin has cabin fever and we visit our friends, one after another, to drown out the wind with conversation. There is only one topic: the wind. We compare predictions, weather forecasts, barometer readings, and temperatures. Today is noticeably colder. The kitchen door is bolted shut and Freda stuffs the cracks with rags to cut down on drafts. The kerosene heater now stays lighted day and night and just manages to keep off the chill.

On the fifth and sixth days, though it continues to grow colder, nothing much changes. The barometer has stopped dropping and is low but steady. Anxiety and irritability increase. We consider leaving the basin but decide to stick it out. It can't go on much longer. We barricade ourselves against the noise, vibration, and cold in the parlor by the fire, waiting. Old timers are saying "maybe it's the end of the season. Another few days and we'll have frost. Even if it stops, the summer won't recover." Everyone complains of wakefulness, nightmares, and grouchy companions.

On the seventh day the barometer begins to rise and the radio forecasts "lessening winds in the high mountains." The basin is waiting and tense as the magic hour of sunset approaches, but nightfall brings no relief. We settle down for the evening with books before the fire, but after an hour we become aware of a change: instead of constant wind we have a series of gusts, and between the gusts it is almost still! We exchange hopeful glances and cross our fingers. An hour later the lulls are noticeably longer. By the time we go to bed there is only an occasional gust. Late in the night, awakened by the unaccustomed stillness, I notice Freda is awake. "It's over," she says gratefully and goes back to sleep. I lie awake awhile to savor the quiet.

In the morning we sleep late until awakened by sounds of activity on the lake. Motorboats, rowboats, taxis, and canoes are full of people celebrating the end of the blow. By midmorning the air is miraculously warm. Fishermen are trolling, cabin-owners head for the Chalet to shop, and kids are playing in the shallows despite a ten-degree drop in the water temperature. There is an air of rejoicing and thanksgiving. The barometer has risen sharply and billowing clouds, the first in a week, sail over the basin on an afternoon breeze that obligingly dies at sunset.

149

Canoeing after dinner we can hear the splash of rising trout in the stillness. The seven-day ordeal, though not forgotten, is behind us.

Once or twice in a decade a really big rainstorm with continuous wind somehow slips past the offshore high pressure barricade and descends on Granite Basin. With wind to drive the rain it is almost impossible to keep dry, and after a few days even the bluejays and squirrels are wet and bedraggled. Leaks develop in the cabin in familiar spots: down the kitchen stovepipe, along the pantry north wall, and there are drips above the loft stairs and in the middle of the loft double bed. Since substantial rains are rare, and most leaks swell closed in a day or so, I have never bothered to find the sources of our drips.

The last big storm that swept Granite Basin brought the lake up a foot, flooded the channel, filled the snowpool and caused the cataract beneath the house to wash out a footing beneath the bay. The resulting four-inch sag broke a window. In the first three savage days, the wind and rain were so heavy that three backcountry campers died of exposure in their effort to escape. And the wilderness was empty before the fourth consecutive night of rain.

Rainstorms can materialize with amazing suddenness. One minute the sky is clear, the next minute it's raining. Often there's no overcast period in between. Once I was canoeing under what I thought were cloudless skies when it suddenly seemed that all around me small trout were rising. It wasn't until one of the raindrops struck me that I realized what was happening. Another time I was lazily sailing, gazing off down the basin at distant clouds, when a clap of thunder almost knocked me from the boat. I turned to see black thunderheads boiling close behind me. Aware that my nineteen-foot aluminum mast would make a perfect lightning rod, I headed for the harbor. It was raining before I could take down the sail.

Another boating misadventure had its roots in undue optimism. It was late in June, a blow had begun, and we were almost out of milk for Kath, still a baby. Windblasted whitecaps covered the lake, but I wasn't in the mood for a five-mile walk and I thought I could make it by boat to the Chalet. Rafferty, as usual, insisted on coming. The waves in Lower Granite were the biggest I had seen, but I set my speed to match that of the combers and headed straight down the middle of the lake. Though the waves were predictable the strong cross wind wasn't, and I was forced to speed up to maintain steerage and keep from broaching.

The boat would ride one big wave until it topped the crest, then fall sickeningly to the bottom of the deep trough beyond, the water gurgling and boiling high around us on all sides. Just when the walls of water seemed about to bury us, the boat would be picked up and borne forward again on another giant swell. Raff looked at me imploringly, his wet ears flattened back, but there was nothing to do except hang on and keep going. Before we reached the Chalet's sheltered harbor, we had surfed through waves that must have measured five feet from trough to crest.

By the time we were ready to return the wind had lessened, and the swells, while still huge, were no longer topped with foam. Getting back up the lake seemed feasible enough, so I cradled the carton of milk in a lifejacket, and we set forth. The waves, of course, were worse than they looked and the buffeting was terrific, but before we were five hundred yards beyond the harbor the engine quit and no amount of cranking would induce it to start.

Wind and waves drove us back toward the Chalet, the boat bobbing like a cork, and I helped them along by standing and spreading my slicker like a sail. I had second thoughts, however, when I saw how the rollers were breaking across the stone jetty ahead. Fortunately Bruce, the dock boss, had spotted the drifting boat and came out to tow us back into the harbor. Though he got the engine running, the ignition was fouled and only one cylinder was firing, which meant we couldn't run at slow speed. Bruce doubted the engine would get me up the lake, but I thought I could make it and again we set forth.

The engine sounded feeble and when the storm drowned out its sound I knew it was dying and opened the throttle wide. The bow would shoot up and hang in the air before falling back, but yard by yard we made our way up the lake. Clearing a point put us into the worst of the storm for several minutes. The lake was a chaos of froth and stinging spray, and it was coming so fast I couldn't open my eyes in the face of the wind. As the boat leaped and skittered, Raff began to whine.

We crashed down so hard from one of our leaps that the seat broke beneath me, throwing me backward, but I clung to the wheel and struggled to a kneeling position on the wreckage. A minute later the driving spray lessened and I opened my eyes. The channel was only a hundred yards away. But when we reached it I remembered I couldn't slow down or the motor would die. That was the fastest trip I ever made between the lakes, hanging out of the boat to help bank the sharp turns as I shot beneath the overhanging trees. When the boat was in its berth and I was tying the lines, Rafferty gave thanks by eagerly licking my face. Then, I remembered the milk. The carton had come loose from its cushioning preserver and was floating in six inches of oily water in the stern, but miraculously it was intact!

Every fall, usually in late October, after a period of stormy weather the lakes undergo a strange transformation. I wake up one quiet, cold morning to discover that yesterday's clear water has turned muddy and roiled. A rusty looking oil slick covers much of the surface, and rotten twigs and needles, often covered with slime, float everywhere. Though the air is still the water appears to be quietly churning, and debris moves about on strange currents. Here and there bubbles rise and break on the surface, and there's an odor of mudflats and rotting vegetation.

What I had seen, I later learned, was the annual autumn temperature inversion, when the water in the lake quite literally turns over. It's a peculiar fact that water is heavier at forty degrees Fahrenheit than it is when it's warmer or colder.

During the summer all the water in both lakes is warmer than forty degrees, but sometime in late October shorter days and fall storms cool the surface to the critical temperature. When this happens the heavy surface water sinks to the bottom and the warmer bottom water rises to the top. The currents produced as the lakes turn upside down lift debris off the bottom and bring it boiling to the surface. Happily, the condition is only temporary. The waterlogged debris sinks back to the bottom long before the ice can trap it for the winter.

Probably the most dramatic weather change I've witnessed occurred in a rare February drought. There hadn't been a decent snowstorm in nearly three months and it was almost like summer on snowless Star Peak. Because the Pacific high-pressure area was well entrenched and fending off all storms, and the forecast called for continued fair weather, I arrived without snowshoes, skis or heavy clothing. I was able to drive almost a mile up the unploughed road to the basin and park on a patch of bare pavement.

When I reached the cabin, a little past sunset, I was shocked to find the hollow in which it nestled had become a lake of solid ice, in places three feet thick, its surface just two inches from the floor joists. My buried gas pipe, I felt sure, must be broken again, and when I lifted the hatch in the parlor floor I found the valve completely embedded in ice. With water boiled on a kerosene stove I melted enough ice to free the valve and turn it on. To my surprise gas came on in the stove with normal pressure. If the pipe was broken the ice was sealing in the gas.

That night after dinner I walked up the frozen upper lake by the light of a sickle moon to visit Mike, now the resident winter patrolman, at his cabin by the Scout camp. Together we deduced how the ice field beneath my cabin had formed. Late in the fall a freak heavy rainstorm had filled the snowpool above the outhouse and set the stream running beneath the cabin. Then the brimming pool had frozen over. In the unseasonably warm weather that followed, daily snowmelt in the pool's watershed had been sufficient to keep the stream running beneath its covering of ice and snow.

Running streams in midwinter go through a daily cycle. During the coldest hours of the night, white anchor ice forms along the margins and the streambed, causing the water to rise. During the day, the sun melts the ice and the water level drops back to normal. But in the darkness beneath the cabin the process was interrupted. The anchor ice, instead of melting, grew thicker, and the accumulation formed a dam that spread out the flow beneath the cabin. The dam grew wider and wider until it reached beyond the cabin to the nearby granite walls of the hollow. When the hollow was dammed water began to back up behind the cabin. Now the frozen lake extended sixty feet up the draw!

I wondered if the growing pool of ice could lift the cabin.

Mike was sure it couldn't, because the ice exerted no upward force, but he agreed it could rise around the cabin and work its way inside. When I returned to the cabin later that evening I could hear running water in the stillness. Since none of it was reaching the mouth of the cove, the dam was intact and the ice field behind it still growing. Before I went to bed I checked the barometer and found the pressure high (30.35) as expected.

The following morning the glass had dropped two full points, and a breeze began to grow as I made up my pack for a day on Star Peak. It was too windy on the summit to finish my lunch, and I descended in a freezing late-afternoon wind to find the barometer had dropped another point, to 29.95.

At sunset I bucked a stiff headwind to join Mike for dinner, followed by a luxurious hot shower. He told me the radio forecast called for wind all night and heavy snow beginning about noon the next day. The wind was stronger as I made my way home across the ice and lit a fire. The sky was still clear but in four hours the glass had dropped to 29.72, the lowest reading I'd ever seen in the basin. Anticipating the need for an early departure, I made up my pack, laid out breakfast, and readied the cabin before going to bed.

When I awoke to the grey of a stormy dawn, the wind was still blowing and a heavy snow was falling. The barometer was down to an alarming 29.55, culminating an incredible drop of eight full points in little more than thirty-six hours! I quickly closed the cabin and set forth on foot down the lake dressed in all the clothing I had been able to find. The wind was at my back, propelling me along, and since the footing was good my progress was excellent. Visibility was poor in the blowing snow, but I managed to keep the south shore in view.

I was entering the harbor, only fifty feet from shore, beginning to think about my snowbound car, when the ice gave away beneath me and I sank like a rock. Luckily the water was only three feet deep. I broke away the thin ice in the hole with my arms, then threw myself on what I hoped was strong ice and rolled free of the water. Scrambling to my feet, I climbed out of the harbor and up the hill behind it, moving fast to ward off the chill. Half a mile brought me to the car and I hurriedly brushed off the foot of snow that covered it. The starter cranked the engine very slowly in the cold, and I remembered the battery had one bad cell, but the engine finally caught.

By then my trousers were frozen stiff and I was starting to shiver. I feared I might freeze if I stopped to put on chains, so I decided to risk getting stuck in the snow. Hanging my head out the window to see, concentrating hard on staying in the ruts, I slithered my way through a mile of deep snow to the highway. Conditions there were not much better, but after a cold and nerve-wracking hour the road was free of snow and I could safely stop to shed my squishing boots and put on dry socks. By then the worst was past, but my legs did not get warm until the storm in Granite Basin lay more than a hundred miles behind me. For once I'd had enough dramatic weather.

TEN

Winter at the Cabin

In the basin the boundary between winter and fall is easily the most elusive seasonal change. It is impossible to tell if the snow that falls in a Thanksgiving storm will form the base for a pack that will last seven months, or if the last of it will melt in a week of late-autumn warm weather. One still-as-death morning in early December Lower Granite may be filmed with a mirrorlike sheet of paper-thin ice that shatters in the first morning breeze and disappears. But if the breeze fails to rise and the ice survives the weak midday sun, it will grow thicker in the long freezing night and be twice as hard to shatter or melt the next day.

During the transition from autumn to winter travel in the basin is at its most difficult. Even the hardiest find it more convenient to be elsewhere. The Chalet has been closed for more than a month, the lakes are down, and the last of the boats should have been pulled from the rocky harbor and stored under roofs where the dependably heavy snows cannot crush them. (Each year, somewhere in the basin, a boat is forgotten or its owner is delayed in returning, and we find the ruins in the spring.) Outboard motors have long since been drained before freezing nights can crack their water-cooled jackets.

By mid-November the road from the highway is generally closed by snow, but rocks, open pavement and uncompacted powder prevent easy use of snowshoes or skis. Since the boats are put away the only access to cabins is by trail, which by this time is drifted over with snow that conceals the oil-slick ice of frozen puddles.

Winter arrives, by my calculation, when permanent ice covers all—or nearly all—of Lower Granite. That can be anytime between early December and late January. A succession of cold early storms so chilled the basin one year that ice began to form along the lower lake's shore well before Thanksgiving. And I have more than once crossed on green and bending ice a week before Christmas. Jorgy's rule of thumb is "stay off the ice until the New Year begins," but his young daughters were usually out skating before Christmas.

At the other extreme, mild temperatures extended autumn well into December one year, and on the tenth of the month I drove a motorboat up the lower lake. The day was so warm that I took off my shirt in the sun though I had to break ice in the harbor. Mermaid Cove was still open water and inhabited by sea gulls well into February, and we thought for a while it might not freeze at all that winter.

A strange phenomenon that same year was the presence of two holes about fifty yards apart in the ice, each three or four yards across, near the middle of Lower Granite. Springs in the lake bottom or escaping subterranean air apparently kept the water from freezing well past the time when the rest of the ice was safe for travel. Those two black holes in the snow-covered ice persisted into February, then gradually closed and disappeared beneath the snow. But skiing down the lake in their vicinity a month later, I wondered about the thickness of their now hidden ice.

Upper Granite usually freezes two to five weeks before permanent ice covers the lower lake. Since it is only a fifth as large, shallower and broken by islands, its surface waters cool more quickly. Its ice is better protected from the wind, and its higher sheltering ridges provide more shade from the low-lying winter sun. I have often seen its entire surface glazed with shiny new ice in early November, and our cove is sometimes frozen in late October.

Freda's first winter trip to the basin came the second year we owned the cabin. Jorgy had called a few days after Christmas to invite us to stay in his cabin and see the new ice before it was covered with snow. There hadn't been a storm since early November and, except for the frozen lake, he said it looked like fall. This had been his first Christmas without snow on the ground. Even the road from the highway was open.

The lake, when we arrived, was like a sheet of mildly polished steel, and half a dozen children were skating and playing in what was left of the sunlight along the eastern shore. Freda went up to Jorgy's cabin to get warm while I crossed the empty spillway and started up the lake on the snow-free trail. I made very good time in the crisp, still air on ice-cemented gravel that crunched beneath my boots.

After perhaps a mile, I climbed down off the trail and walked out on the ice. It was black and transparent but filled with small imprisoned bubbles that gave it the look of frozen champagne. Sidelighted by the last of the sinking sun, the tiny bubbles glowed like pearls against the blackness beneath.

The unyielding solidity of the ice soon gave me confidence, and before long I discovered that once I got running I could plant my feet and slide a good distance, even with rubber-soled boots. Before I knew it I was halfway across the lake. The channel mouth looked close and I thought I could make it, but then the sun went down and suddenly it was cold. With the open water at the head of the lake only a hundred yards distant, it occurred to me that the ice I was sliding on might be quite thin.

Almost as soon as the sunlight disappeared the ice, which until then had been as still as concrete, began to shiver and make all manner of sounds. As happens in midwinter darkness came swiftly, and all at once I felt extremely vulnerable. I turned and started running toward the nearest point of land as fracture lines zigzagged past me and the ice groaned and shook as though ready to shatter. It was easy to imagine a crack opening beneath my feet then abruptly closing above me!

When I had nearly reached shore I realized someone was calling. It was Freda who, once she was warm, had followed me up the trail and spotted me out on the ice. By the time I joined her the growling of the ice seemed less sinister. Though we hurried down the trail it was absolutely black before we groped our way to Jorgy's kitchen for dinner.

The following morning after breakfast we packed a lunch and headed for the cabin. Clouds had come in during the night to

chill the basin, but they sailed off to the south in an early morning breeze and by the time we reached the trail the sky was sunny and still. The warming day made the restless ice protest, and as we moved along we cataloged its impressive variety of sounds.

Freda was understandably unwilling to take the shortcut across the ice, so we kept to the trail that circles the lake. In sunny Mermaid Cove we stopped to eat lunch on a sloping granite slab. Behind us the cliff was so thick with ice it resembled a quick-frozen waterfall. In pockets of earth in the rock at our feet, freezing water extruded upward, formed tiny white mushrooms so delicate they shattered when we touched them.

When at last we reached the cabin it might have been the day we closed up in late September, except that the stream, always dry in the fall, was a broad strip of ice that stretched from the outhouse to the lake. A cloudburst had filled the snowpond to overflowing, and before it could empty the stream had frozen solid in its bed. The upper lake ice had twisted the pier's outer span into an "S," but there was nothing whatever to be done. It would stay that way another five months until the breakup released it—or completed its destruction.

We unlocked the cabin and I turned on the flamo, lit the stove, and set the teakettle boiling with water dipped from the channel. Once the tea was ready we took our steaming mugs outside to the porch where the temperature was twenty degrees warmer. It was nice to return to our cabin in the mountains, if only to drink tea on its porch on New Year's Eve.

Three years later, almost to the day, conditions were quite different. It had been storming for two weeks and the forecast was for continued heavy weather. After a hectic holiday season I was anxious to get away to the snowbound solitude of Granite, so I called Jorgy and suggested a trip to the basin. He had no interest in fighting his way through a blizzard and urged me to wait until the weather cleared. But I didn't want to wait, and I didn't really want company. After dozens of winter trips with Jorgy, I was ready to try it alone. When he saw I meant to go he warned me to keep a close watch for thin ice and open water, since the ice was still green despite the long storm.

It was late afternoon, only an hour before nightfall, when I reached the Granite turnoff and parked the car against a snow-bank. A heavy snow was falling through the grey windless sky, but visibility was good. Warmly dressed, and carrying a small pack, I skied up the road without difficulty. But when I climbed through the pass that led down to the lake, I met a stiff wind that blew snow in my eyes. After stopping to put on goggles, I cautiously picked my way down the steep slope to the harbor and started up the lake on the snow-covered ice.

The wind was stronger on the lake, and the blowing snow cut visibility to less than fifty feet. As the afternoon light began to fade I wished I had gotten an earlier start, although my progress so far had been excellent. Head down, leaning forward, I skied straight into the wind, roughly following the southern shore. All I could see through the swirling cloud was the shadowy line of trees on my left. After perhaps a quarter-mile, bare ice began to show through the covering of snow, and I found myself zigzagging from one snow patch to another to avoid the slippery surface.

Soon the last of the snow was gone, and before I set forth on the treacherous ice I stopped to get my bearings. But the trees had disappeared. I had moved too far out onto the ice. All I could see was the ice beneath my feet and the swirling snow around me. There was nothing to guide me but the wind, which I hoped was still blowing down the basin. Moving upwind on bare ice proved extremely difficult. The dull edges of my skis and blunt tips of my poles gave me very little purchase, and I fell repeatedly.

I switched to a sidestep, then changed to a herringbone, but while I fell less often my progress was too slow. I tried digging in the inside edges of my skis and relying on my arms for propulsion, but if a pole tip slipped I always fell. The afternoon was growing darker and I had no idea how far I'd come. My goggles were plastered with the blowing snow and I found myself continually cleaning them. Finally, in exasperation, I stuffed them in my pocket, but the blinding snow that quickly crusted my face forced me to put them back on.

Stopping for a moment to wipe the snow from my glasses, I looked down in horror to see the tips of my skis suspended over black open water! For a moment I was too shocked to move. One more blind step would have put me in the lake. In my struggle with the ice and blowing snow I'd completely forgotten Jorgy's warning. I ripped off my goggles and looked carefully around. The ice behind and to the sides seemed intact, but I knew it must be very thin. Without lifting my feet I gingerly slipped backwards, away from that terrifying blackness. Then shielding my eyes I stared hard at where the shore should be.

After half a minute, in a lull between gusts, I thought I detected a darkness that might be trees. Bent almost double to scrutinize the ice, jabbing hard with my poles, I circled in that direction, away from the awful open water. Within twenty-five yards I was back again on snow and climbing toward shoreline I could now clearly see. I didn't care where I was. All I could think of was getting off the ice. But once on shore, my relief was shortlived. Darkness was coming fast and I had no idea where I was.

With all the speed I could muster I skied up the shore, crashing through brush, squeezing between trees, slipping and falling on ice-encrusted rocks. Then I spotted a cabin and gratefully rushed toward it, planning to break in and bivouac for the night. But by the time I reached it there were others in sight and I decided to continue a little farther before quitting. After I had passed four cabins the going got easier and I began to have some feeling for where I was. Unfortunately, darkness was only minutes away. Then ahead through the trees I glimpsed a lighter area. It might be the lake, or it might be the open granite ledge beside the channel. I decided to find out before breaking in for the night.

When I came out of the trees I was on the hoped-for ledge, and a line of trees ahead marked the channel. The cabin lay only a quarter mile away and I knew I could make it. Although by now it was dark I felt confident and strong. I moved quickly down the ledge and splashed through the channel's shallow water. There was just enough light when I got to the cabin to locate the outhouse and turn on the gas before taking off my skis and letting myself into the kitchen.

I lighted a lamp, turned on the gas heater, and put on water to heat. Then, overwrought by my narrow escape, I paced the warming kitchen for an hour, drinking coffee, before it occurred to me to change my soaked clothes and think about dinner.

The following day, after a night of restless dreams, the sky was clear but a cold wind was blowing. Largely out of habit I patrolled Upper Granite, following the shoreline and keeping a close lookout for open water. The ice here seemed thicker and was totally covered with snow. At the head of the lake, just above the upper landing, I found the little shack that houses the upper lake phone. Taking off my skis and using one of them as a shovel, I dug my way inside. It was cold and dark and partly filled with snow, but a hum in the phone meant the line was intact. I called Freda, collect, as promised, to let her know I had safely arrived.

The following day, refreshed by my visit, I closed the cabin and headed down the basin. The day was so perfect, sunny and clear, that it was hard to believe I had been lost in a storm only forty-five hours before. The lower lake ice was now covered with snow and I crossed it with confidence, keeping well away from the shore. But I felt compelled to find that gaping hole in the ice. The four cabins I had passed were easily found, and they led me, in turn, to a shallow rocky cove, undoubtedly the spot where I beheld the dark water, though now there was none to be seen. The spot looked innocent enough in the cheerful mid-day sunshine, but I kept my distance as I continued my journey down the lake.

With that trip behind me, I no longer thought twice about visiting the cabin by myself, in any season. But never again have I deliberately crossed the basin alone in a blizzard. After that trip I filed sharp edges on my skis and ground points on my ski poles. I also added a pair of sharp six inch nails to my winter kit. Theoretically they allow a person fallen through thin ice to claw his way out of the water. That's one theory I hope never to test.

Two winters later I encountered a new hazard while making my way up Lower Granite. It was a still, clear day—until the distant clatter of a helicopter sounded somewhere up the basin. In a moment I spotted the little ship approaching from the back-country. It was flying low and following the trail, apparently searching for a party reported lost or overdue. The ship crossed Upper Granite, climbed to clear the trees above the channel, then spotted me.

It immediately changed course and headed my way, cruising no more than twenty feet above the ice, its turbulence creating a snowstorm as it came. I stopped and waited for it to veer away, but instead it dropped lower as though to run me down. Just before its slipstream spun me around and covered me with swirl-ing snow, I saw a man beside the pilot with a rifle on his knees studying me intently through binoculars. The ship passed so close I had to drop to the ice to avoid being hit, and I swore as it continued down the basin. Later I learned the police had been looking for an escaped murderer whose path reportedly led to the basin. He was thought to be hiding in an upper lake cabin. I'm pleased to say it wasn't mine.

A month or two later I was skiing down the lake in a snow-storm so heavy that visibility was less than ten feet. The wind was at my back, pushing me along, and I was sure there was no open water to surprise me. All at once, above the wind, I heard the voices of two women in casual conversation. I moved toward the sound and two shadowy forms appeared on my right. From their voices I recognized them as neighbors from the head of Lower Granite. They were intently discussing chicken casserole seasonings. Having nothing to contribute, I saw no reason to intrude. Like me, they doubtless believed themselves alone. I skied on past without being seen.

Just after New Year's the following winter, I skied up the lake with a friend named Bill to close up the cabin before it filled with snow. Jorgy had called two days before to report I'd forgotten to put away the canoe. He'd dug it from the snow and dragged it to the cabin, where he found the kitchen door blown open. He'd managed to shove the canoe inside but the door had failed to shut, and he urged me to get there as soon as I could.

Reaching the cabin late one stormy afternoon we turned on the gas and entered through the loft. The kitchen was a mess. The ice-encrusted canoe sat on a two-foot-deep snowdrift that covered every inch of the floor, and snow was still blowing in through the two-inch gap in the doorway. The table and couch were covered with snow and the chairs were frozen to the floor. It was hard to know where to begin.

After lighting the 20,000 BTU heater in the stove, we emptied the canoe of snow and ice, dragged it outside, and carried it up to its accustomed place in the loft. Then, between mugs of coffee, we attacked the drifted floor with shovels. In less than an hour both rooms were free of snow, but hidden beneath it, we discovered with dismay, was an inch of hard ice tightly frozen to the floor!

It refused to be pried loose with a flat-bladed shovel and it failed to shatter when struck a sharp blow. (The floor still shows the scars from our attempts.) As darkness approached and the wind grew stronger, we turned our attention to getting the door closed. Since we were going to have to spend the night in that icebox we had to stop the snow from blowing in. Using hammers and screw drivers, we chiseled away ice, but even when the door and the jamb were clean, the door was too swollen to close. Finally we drove it in place with hammers and nailed it securely for the winter. By then it was dark so we quit to light lanterns and fix dinner.

I slept that night on a bare spot in front of the stove while Bill spread his mummy bag on the frosty couch. Although the gas heater ran full blast all night, the sheet of ice on the floor kept the room just ten degrees above freezing. In the morning after breakfast we tried a new approach. After cracking the ice with hammers we poured on boiling water, then quickly pried up a loosened section with the shovel. When this procedure worked we turned on all four burners and covered the stove top with kettles.

Soon the floor was awash and the air was white with steam. Gradually the sheet of ice shrank and by noon it was gone. Then we switched to mops and towels to soak up the room full of water. It was as humid as a sauna but the blowing snow outside kept us from opening a window. When most of the water had been squeezed into the sink, we quit and hastily packed to leave. Another night in that room was unthinkable! Outside in the snowstorm it seemed marvelously dry, and we enjoyed our trip down the lake to the car. When I returned a month later, not knowing what I'd find, the cabin was perfectly dry.

Midwinter days spent alone in the basin are among the most peaceful I have ever known. A Saturday in late February, sunny and still, was fairly typical. At 9 a.m. the temperature on the shaded back porch was only twelve degrees, but a few yards away on the bare granite bluff, to which I'd carried my breakfast, it was so hot in the sun I immediately took off my shirt.

The lake was a dazzling sunlit mirror and the morning was so still the silence seemed tangible. Living in the city we are usually unaware of background noise until all at once it is missing. Sitting in the brilliant morning silence on that rock, I could hear, very clearly, the sound of my breathing. And when I brought out my notebook the sound of the ballpoint on paper was distinct.

Out on the ice I noticed a black speck. I assumed it was a rock or a pine cone, until it moved. I made Indian sunglasses—narrow slits between my fingers—but I still couldn't tell what it was, so I went inside for binoculars. The moving spot was a young porcupine, which should have been hibernating. Apparently something had disturbed its sleep or invaded its lair, and now it was aimlessly plodding on the ice, going one way then another, changing direction for no apparent reason. It seemed to be thoroughly confused.

When five skiers appeared from behind an island, heading straight for the porcupine, I quickly put on snowshoes and hurried out onto the lake. Coming up behind the lumbering beast I gently herded him off the ice and into the timber. He moved unhurridly into the forest's cool shade, the quills of his tail rustling quietly on the snow. Then he calmly selected a thirty foot lodgepole and methodically climbed until he was hidden among the highest branches. The skiers, who passed by talking, never saw him.

After a party of mountaineers came up the lake an hour later the basin began to feel crowded, so I decided to spend the rest of the day on Star Peak. In my knapsack I packed a nylon parka shell, a first-aid kit and my lunch. Then, aiming just to the west of Red Hill, I started up, shirtless, on snowshoes. In the winter when trails and brush, boulders and deadfalls are all buried six to twelve feet beneath the snow one can travel in comparatively straight lines on snowshoes, even where the slope is quite steep.

After passing the just-protruding tops of the redwood water-tanks, I headed up a route that would have been difficult in summer. The snow was in excellent condition for showshoeing, although I wished I had thought to bring ski poles. When I reached the ridge the sage plain that led to the summit was nearly bare, and I was happy to shed my snowshoes and walk the rest of the way on rock.

In the summit rocks, I found a tiny hollow half-filled with fresh water, which I fed with handfuls of snow, stirring briskly, until there was enough for a drink. Then I removed my sweaty clothes, carefully anchoring them with rocks, to enjoy the mild breeze and bright sun. While eating my lunch I examined the blue dripping cornice beside me and the smoothly frosted ranges that lay in all directions, then I lay down for a nap in a sheltered, gravel-floored hollow, and slept.

When it was time to go the descent was beautiful and swift. After returning to my snowshoes I turned east on wind-sculpted snow through the open timber of the park. I was probably its

first visitor in six months. In the yellow light of late afternoon
the little hanging valley seemed to glow. By the time I half-
walked, half-slid down a steep snow gulley to the ramp, the far
side of the basin was already in shadow. As I continued down I
watched the shadows advance across the basin and climb up to
meet me. We met as I passed Red Hill.

By the time I reached the cabin, after a day alone, I was ready
for company. The day before on the way to the cabin I had
encountered Bill and Galen, each with his daughter, on the way
to their adjacent upper lake cabins. They had invited me to visit
so I put an icy bottle of sherry in my pack and snowshoed up the
lake to Galen's cabin, where I found the four of them assembled
around the glowing wood stove. Before finishing the sherry we
decided to pool our food for dinner, and in the last of the light
Bill and I returned to our cabins for the ingredients.

Back in Galen's kitchen, while the girls played cards and Bill
snored by the stove, Galen and I set to work on dinner. Into a
heavy skillet on the old kitchen range we emptied half-frozen
cans of kidney beans, tamales, lima beans and diced mushrooms.
To this we added a chopped white onion, a pound of fresh
hamburger and a sprinkling of spices and herbs. While this
mixture gently simmered, we emptied cans of peaches, apricots,
and pears over fresh-cut apple and banana, then stirred in a pint
of cottage cheese. Our hunger and the sherry may have influ-
enced our judgment, but this two-dish dinner seemed a feast.

***

After traveling to the cabin for several years on snowshoes or
skis borrowed from Jorgy, I bought myself a pair of Scandanavian
cross-country skis. The first time I wore them they felt so narrow
they seemed more like ice skates, and my ankles turned with
disconcerting ease, but they took me up the basin with surprising speed. I was sailing along in the middle of the lake when I
heard a shout of alarm. A skier with a large pack was laboriously
traversing the steep drift of snow that covered the rocky south
shore.

"Get off the ice!" he yelled. "It's dangerous!"

He seemed highly excited, so I skied closer to find out why. He repeated his injunction with great agitation, as though the ice was about to part beneath me. I assured him the lake, well away from warm rocks, was perfectly safe, and even the occasional patches of slush were only ten inches deep and floored with hard ice.

"Like hell!" he retorted. "I just fell four feet through a crack! I nearly went in the lake!" The experience had understandably unnerved him. When I asked where this had happened he pointed out the cove where I had so nearly fallen in myself, years before. I tried to explain why the shoreline was more dangerous than the middle of the lake, but anxiety had made him angry and he told me I was crazy. As I continued up the lake I stopped from time to time to look back and make sure he hadn't fallen in another hidden crack, and I have no doubt that he watched me, too. Before I entered the trees at the head of the lake I took a last look for the man who had tried his best to save me. I could see a black dot approaching the Chalet, so both of us had made it. Despite the interruption that first trip up the basin on cross-country skis was the fastest I had ever made.

Conditions at the cabin were normal for April. The motorboat, its hull to the wind, still stood on its transom, lashed between two trees, and juncos were feeding on the patch of bare ground in its lee. Kath's swing, which sails out over the water of the cove in summer, had as usual been flung into the trees by the wind. The granite bluff, between the cabin and ice, was bare and dry, while behind the cabin drifts rose halfway up the roof. Hungry jays were squawking in the trees and somewhere up the lake a grouse was drumming.

I was hot from the trip and once inside the cabin I shed all my clothes and took a can of cold beer to the loft porch overlooking the lake. Beer is a staple in weather like this, but I have learned the hard way to stock the cabin with nothing but aluminum cans. Bottles explode and bi-metal cans sometimes pop when they freeze. The can from which I drank was so round on the bottom it refused to stand, evidence that earlier in the winter it had frozen.

* * *

In the first few years after the fireplace was constructed I used to dread building fires after a period of heavy snow, because I knew the chimney would be blocked. Bat had assured me snow would be "no problem." I only wish he had been there the stormy January night I found the steel damper frozen shut. By kicking hard on the handle, I finally got it open an inch, then by lantern light I laid a fire and doused it heavily with kerosene. Before striking a match I built a log roof that I hoped would shield the flames from melting snow above.

When the kerosene caught, most of the flame and all of the smoke billowed out into the parlor. I lay flat on the floor as the room filled with smoke, helpless to do anything but watch. The heavy storm outside prevented me from opening the windows. Occasionally I gave the damper handle a kick, and bit by bit it opened as heat from below thawed the ice. By the time the chimney was beginning to draw the cabin was thick with smoke and I could stand it no longer. Choking, eyes streaming, I ran out into the night for fresh air. Then despite the blowing snow I threw open doors and windows to let the wind drive out the smoke.

Ten minutes later I ventured back inside to find the air clear, the fire burning brightly and the chimney drawing well. But my problems were not over. Snowmelt and slush were pouring down the chimney, bombarding my makeshift roof and threatening to put out the fire. I redoubled the roof, but by that time black water was pouring across the hearth into the room. I ran to the kitchen and returned with two big kettles and a sponge. One kettle I positioned on the roof above the fire, where it would catch the main stream; the other I used as a basin for the water I mopped up with the sponge.

For nearly half an hour I barely kept the inky flood from reaching the mattress in front of the hearth. Meanwhile, the fire was spitting and hissing as the deluge found its way through the sodden log roof and seeped through the ashes to live coals. Not until the middle of the evening had the last of the snow in the chimney melted and the fireplace finally became dry.

It was evident I needed some sort of a cap that would keep out the snow while letting out smoke. The following summer I found an old tinsmith who knew what I wanted and built me an intricately baffled bonnet that he swore would not impair the chimney's draw. I had to chisel out the top row of rocks that faced the fireplace to make it fit, but it has worked so well I no longer even need close the damper.

It is my custom in winter to spend days in the kitchen and evenings in the parlor. The kitchen has large windows on three sides which catch the sun and warm the room, but they also chill the room swiftly at night. The parlor, buried as it is beneath drifted snow, is cold and dark during the day, but at night it becomes a cozy den. When I come in from my late afternoon tour, I light a fire in the fireplace to start warming up the parlor, while I cook my dinner in the still sun-warmed kitchen.

The moment dinner is ready, I take it in by the fire. Once I close off the kitchen and lower the hatch to seal off the loft, I am ready to light the big candles on the mantle and settle myself for a leisurely and comfortable meal.

After dinner I usually sink back in the big overstuffed leather rocker or stretch out, propped by pillows, on the canvas-covered mattress by the hearth. One of my delights on those long winter evenings is simply drinking the water. In the city I shun water but in the basin I find myself drinking glass after glass. Partly, of course, it's because the dry air promotes dehydration, but also it's because the basin's water has a marvelous flavor. I always miss it when I leave in the fall, and so does Kath. She suggests we fill big bottles and take them home for the winter, but I doubt the flavor would survive.

Winter water can be a problem in the basin. Cabin owners who ski in for the weekend must come to the channel, Granite Creek, or Rainbow Creek to be sure of a supply. The few who stay longer sometimes saw or chop holes in the ice. I am fortunate to be only fifty yards from the channel, though I sometimes must break an inch or two of ice.

If the night is still and a moon is up, I make it a point to go out for a stroll on the ice. Even a quarter moon lights the white bowl so well that once my eyes adjust I can travel in safety without a flashlight—as long as I keep clear of the shadows of trees. The wind-packed covering of snow is often frozen so hard that I need neither snowshoes nor skis.

At first my ears ring with the silence of the night, but before long I begin to hear the dim sounds of grumbling ice, the distant murmur of running water, and perhaps a faint night wind humming in the trees. If I am lucky these soft sounds will be pierced by the calling of coyotes.

If a wind is blowing or the moon is down, instead of going for a walk I go out on the bluff to savor the beauty and wildness and cold. Even without a moon the basin is clearly visible by starlight. In that utterly transparent high-altitude sky it is hard to find a region that isn't thick with stars. One still January night I devised an index to the clarity of the sky. Inside the rough rectangle of the constellation Orion, I counted thirty-three stars. On an unusually clear night in the city a week later, it was a strain to find thirteen!

One moonlit night the coyotes were out in force, and I walked for hours on the rock-hard crust, too excited by the night to go in. Sometime around midnight I came upon Mike and several of our neighbors. They had come out on the ice in the cove just below their cabin to leave the bones from their dinner in the moonlight. I joined them in the cabin and through the window we watched the moonlit cove for coyotes. As we waited, drinking tea, Mike told us of the visit a coyote had paid him a month before.

It had stormed for weeks and except for a tunnel that led to his door, his cabin was a snow mound with only the stovepipe sticking above the drifts. Hungry coyotes had soon grown bold, often coming close in the evening to howl. One morning he discovered tracks on the roof. Then he remembered that he'd burned his garbage the evening before. Drawn by the aroma, coyote had climbed to hungrily sniff the smoking stovepipe.

Though we watched for an hour no animals appeared in the cove before I left. But I heard the next day that the bones had disappeared by morning.

When I return to the cabin from an evening stroll, warmed by the exertion and comfortably tired, I stoke the fire with coal to last through the night, turn off the lantern and crawl into the big foam sleeping bag I like for winter nights. I can go to bed in the seventy-degree room without sweating, yet wake up warm the next morning when the temperature has dropped below freezing.

Snug inside my bag in the curtained, shuttered bay I watch the jumping firelight on the rafters above me, and I smile at the thought that I'm tucked in the hollow of a snowdrift that covers the cabin. I feel like a hibernating bear in his den. I take a last sip of delicious cold water and settle back to listen drowsily to the snapping of the fire and the quiet conversation of the stream beneath the floor.

ELEVEN

Spring

Spring in Granite Basin is a time of great and sudden changes. Long days of almost unbearable heat follow storms from the depths of winter. In the space of perhaps a half-dozen weeks the deep snow gives way to the bare ground of summer. It is a time of almost continuous movement and sound, a restless period of awakening, unfolding, and coming alive. It is dependably wet and sometimes bitterly cold; a time of surprises, not all of them pleasant. But for anyone who loves the mountains it is a wonderful time to be at Granite.

After the short wintry days and long freezing nights, there's relief in the rapidly lengthening days. Most years, snow still blankets the basin in early May, but the sun shines longer than it does in mid-August. I love the constant sound and motion, the deep booming and sharp cracking of restless ice in the night, the calls of feeding birds on a frozen morning, and the endless rush of the stream beneath the cabin. Hardly a night passes without the calling of coyotes. Their restless wailing and barking evokes the urgency of spring.

When the ice begins to move there are exciting new sounds: echoing reports, the splash of splitting icebergs, the deep rumble of grinding blocks that suggests enormous power. As the season progresses and the nights fail to freeze there are the varied and musical sounds of moving water. From across the lake, depending on the wind, comes the pulsating boom of a waterfall under Talking Mountain. From the channel, in the background, I'm aware of the rush of strong current—an altogether different sound from the gurgling underneath the cabin.

173

An occasional sharp tinkling, not unlike breaking glass, marks the shattering of an icicle fallen from the eaves. Everywhere, spawning in ponds and running brooks, the spotted Pacific tree-frog broadcasts his rhythmic *krek-eck*, *krek-eck*, a pulsating din that at its frenzied height overwhelms all other sounds. Warming weather and melting snow bring out the wildlife in force. Robins up from the lowlands compete with chickadees and juncos in the spots of bare ground while hungry golden mantle ground squirrels, fresh from hibernation, fight with squawking bluejays for our food scraps. Across the mouth of Cornell Cove we watch a colony of marmots search for willow buds and the first new grass, their thick furry bodies dark against the granite and snow.

Coyotes, too, are at their boldest in the spring and often descend to the basin floor to hunt. One May afternoon, in response to a low growl from Rafferty, I stepped out on the porch in time to see a large coyote walk disdainfully into our cove on the ice and disappear in the trees without a glance in our direction, though we stood only fifty feet away. On another occasion I watched a handsome pair stroll out of Cornell Cove and disappear up the lake among the islands.

The boundary between seasons is never easy to pinpoint but Spring begins in the basin, according to my reckoning, when the lower lake ice is no longer safe to walk on. My reasoning is simple: heat sufficient to make the ice unstable means winter's grip has finally been broken, even though snow and ice still cover the basin. Depending on the weather and the severity of the winter, the ice becomes unsafe for travel sometime between mid-April and mid-May. The exact time, of course, depends somewhat on the daring, luck, and judgment of the traveler.

The rotting of the ice makes the cabin hard to reach. During the winter months the snow-covered ice offers a direct and level road up the middle of the basin. When this admirable highway begins to grow soft, we are reluctantly forced onto the lake's north shore where we must make our way by trail through alternating stetches of snow, ice, slush, and mud, so we don't give up the ice until we have to.

The lower half of Lower Granite is comparatively safe when the ice begins to rot, because its covering of wind-packed snow

is always thicker. Of course, if warm rains have fallen (and they nearly always have), there will be layers of slush just beneath the frozen crust. Winter thaws or floods produce the same conditions, so the snow is seldom what it seems. There is a sickening feeling when you break through the crust and start to sink in freezing water. But after dropping six inches, or maybe a foot, your skis come to rest on the hard ice beneath, and the only damage—other than perhaps to your nerves—is wet feet.

The upper half of the lake is where the going gets chancy. The first open water in Lower Granite each year, not counting the pool at the mouth of the channel, is along the shallow beach at the head of the lake in Mermaid Cove. The extent of this open water, Jorgy explained, is a valuable index to the condition of the ice. As the pools at the channel and Mermaid Cove grow, so does the danger of crossing between them. If this stretch cannot be crossed we are forced into a long detour, so we try to pass the channel on ice if we can.

I vividly remember one grey afternoon blindly following Jorgy across that treacherous stretch. His ski tracks dissolved into slush before I reached them, and I could hear water spurt as my poles punched through the ice. Sweat poured down my face as I crossed the disintegrating ice, hardly daring to breathe, racing desperately to get across before I sank into the lake. Then suddenly the ice grew hard beneath my skis and I joined Jorgy by the mouth of the channel. Sweating profusely, I looked back at our water-filled tracks in the rippling, gently heaving mass. What kept us up I don't know. If we had slowed for an instant we would have sunk like stones. When I returned to the channel two days later, the area we had crossed was open water.

Two other early spring trips to the cabin were memorable. On the first, snowshoeing alone, I misjudged the condition of the ice that lay concealed beneath fresh snow,. I had gone no more than three hundred yards beyond the harbor when I discovered the ice was badly cracked. There were leads of open water between the floes. Some of the leads were filmed with ice and hidden by a dusting of fresh snow. Instead of retracing my steps to the harbor, I made a second mistake: I decided to traverse the ice to the shore to save the distance I had gained.

Moving cautiously, often hastily withdrawing a sinking foot and changing course, I slowly made my way across the lake, only prevented from falling through at times by the large bridging surface of my snowshoes. When I finally reached the edge of the ice I found a six-foot-wide moat of open water between me and the shore. But this time I played safe. Instead of hunting for an ice bridge, I took off my pack and snowshoes and threw them across, then I jumped. I landed in knee-deep water and waded ashore, grateful to escape with no more than wet boots and trousers.

The other time, I was skiing with Jorgy up the ice along the lower lake's south shore—despite the fact that the northern quarter of the lake was open water. We were traveling side by side when the ice beneath us started to sink. Without noticing it we had skied across a crack and out onto a floe that wasn't big enough to support our combined weight. Jorgy yelled for me to head one way while he scrambled the other. We both escaped the sinking mass before it went under, but our problems continued because the neighboring ice was similarly cracked into water-logged blocks. Keeping well apart and never daring to slow down, we zigzagged our way to shore by skiing nimbly from one sinking ice floe to another.

Experiences like these incline me toward travel by trail in late spring. I know there will be stretches of ice, pools of snowmelt, and steep snowbanks to traverse, but these hazards are small compared to falling through the ice in the middle of the lake. The trail begins at the foot of the lake, crosses the dam and a bridge above the spillway, then climbs in switchbacks a hundred feet above the water before leveling off and heading north up the lakeshore. Despite the difficult short stretches, it is marvelous to be walking up a mountain trail again.

When I reach Mermaid Cove, at the head of the lake, I usually leave the trail, which beyond this point is buried in snow, and descend to the lakeshore on streaming granite slab. Following the top of a stone breakwater and a broad snowless beach, I take a shortcut across the head of the lake to intercept the faint cabin-owner path that descends a quarter-mile to the cabin.

As a rule Lower Granite is open to boats about a week before the upper lake because of its greater size and greater exposure to wind and sun. More than once, following a heavy winter, we have opened the cabin for the summer in midspring with the upper lake ice still intact. One year in late June, after an exceptional winter, the ice was still solid in both lakes when the road was finally ploughed through eight-foot drifts to the Chalet—in late June. We arrived two days later and started up the trail.

Freda, Rafferty, and I carried packs, while Katherine, still a baby, toddled along ahead bundled in a hooded snowsuit. It took us half the day to cover the two miles of snowy trail, sometimes carrying Kath, but the weather was bright and warm and we enjoyed the walk, although Raff, when finally relieved of his pack, rolled happily on his back in the snow.

The cabin had been closed for nine months without a visitor, and it looked it. It took a hammer and a good deal of kicking to force open the buckled front door, after which it refused to close completely for a week. I pried open the shutters and opened the

177

windows, and fresh air and sunlight found their way into the cabin. In an hour it was warm and the musty dampness was replaced by dry mountain air.

A fallen limb had smashed the loft window and a great deal of snow had apparently blown in. Some of it still lay drifted underneath the eaves and, as the cabin warmed, water began to drip through the kitchen ceiling, sizzling and steaming when it hit the stove. With a shovel and a bucket I climbed to the loft and cleaned out the largest of the drifts, and in an hour's time the dripping had stopped.

That night we lay comfortably bundled in bed, across the room from Kath's crib, watching the yellow pattern of intersecting new moons projected on the ceiling from the kerosene heater, listening to the new and exciting sounds of spring: rushing water underneath the floor, the mating chorus of tree-frogs in the snowpool, and the groaning of the restless upper lake ice.

On the last day of June, after nearly a week, the lower lake ice finally broke up. Our supplies were running low so the following day I walked to the Chalet along the nearly dry trail to shop and launch our boat.

By the time I left the harbor a mass of wind-driven ice stretched clear across the foot of the lake, blocking my path. Using the weight of the boat and the power of the motor, I forced my way into a lead in the narrowest part of the pack, and pushed. At first I made good progress, the bow riding up onto a floe then breaking through, but soon the ice jam grew thicker and refused to give way, and my progress stopped. The lane closed behind me and there I sat, motor roaring, stuck in the middle of the pack.

I throttled down and looked around. Though I was locked in the ice, the pack was moving, with ponderous, almost invisible slowness, partly from the pressure of the wind, partly from the thrust of the engine. I increased the power slightly and waited. Gradually the ice floes that held me began to separate. Less than ten minutes from the time I had become icebound I was free of the pack and running smoothly up the middle of the lake through open water. With the ice behind me and the sun shining brightly it seemed almost like summer—which it should have been on the first of July!

During the remainder of that hot, still day the level of the channel rose rapidly as snowmelt poured into the lakes. In the terrific heat of the long afternoon—it was less than two weeks past the year's longest day—several small floes came loose from the upper lake pack and I watched in fascination as they were sucked into the channel to crash against rocks and spin in the eddies of the pools. Before they could reach the lower lake nothing was left but froth and lumps of fast dissolving slush. The Upper Granite breakup was beginning.

It was exciting to watch those ponderous cakes of waterlogged ice gather speed in the current and pound themselves to pieces in the channel. My neighbor Mike, who had come to watch, suggested it might be fun to send more of the ice pack down the chute. The spring breakup, already a month overdue, could use a little help. There were several jutting chunks that looked ready to go if given a little encouragement. Using old oars as poles, we maneuvered the boat to the edge of the pack and set to work opening up a crack. In a minute or two a cake of ice came loose and, after a push to start it on its way, it moved down into the channel.

We watched it past the first bend, then started to chop out a block twice its size. Since it was awkward leaning out of the boat, I put one foot out onto the ice to increase my reach. When I found that the floe held my weight I climbed out to hack more efficiently at the connecting link. But as it broke free it kicked the boat away, and for a minute I was riding the floe toward the channel. Mike started the engine and picked me up before the cake entered the channel on its ride to destruction.

Pleased with our success we ambitiously set to work releasing an iceberg twenty feet long and weighing many tons. This time we beached the boat on the pack and both of us got out, stripped to bathing suits and sneakers, to chop at the rotting ice. When the berg broke loose and started to move we jumped back in the boat, fired up the engine and went to work like a tug maneuvering a large ship. The floe was so long we had to get it pointed downstream before it reached the narrow mouth of the channel. Putting the bow against one end and opening the throttle, we managed to get it turned, but once started the momentum of those tons of waterlogged ice was too great to stop. It continued turning until it ran firmly aground in the shallows just inside the mouth. We thought we had blocked the channel for a week, but by the following morning it was gone.

It was Saturday now and the news that the lower lake ice had finally gone out brought upper lakers up the channel in well-laden outboards and canoes. To their dismay they found the upper lake ice still intact. The motorboats shoved their way up leads into the pack until they got stuck, engines roaring, then the boatmen got out on the ice to chop them free and retreat. One boat backed to the channel, opened the throttle and made a run at the pack, but instead of breaking through it shot up onto the ice, engine screaming, and slid to a halt, the driver looking slightly embarrassed. Shutting off his engine he got out on the ice and shoved the boat back in the water, then he tied to our pier and set off on foot for his cabin with an armload of gear.

Those in canoes were more successful. They would follow a lead until the way was blocked, then get out on the ice and slide their craft across. When they found a new lead they would launch their canoes and paddle off. We watched two canoes far out in the pack moving slowly up the lake in this manner. Now and then we heard a shout as someone stuck a foot through the ice or a boat came close to tipping over. Two other canoes chose to follow a more indirect route around the shore, where the lanes were substantially wider.

One of these pulled up at our pier, and Patty, a hardy young lady in a bikini, stepped out on the ice to cool her feet. One of her companions jokingly suggested that the way to cool off was to jump in the lake. Without hesitation Patty dove neatly through an opening in the ice. She came up wide-eyed and yelling and thrust out her arms to be pulled from the water. Though she was in the water only a matter of seconds, her face still showed the shock five minutes later. She said the cold and the dark had been terrifying.

That night, without a sound, the lake broke up. The combination of daytime heat, rising water, and wind finally overcame the cold that had held the ice in place for seven months. Sometime in the night the huge sheet of ice quietly divided into thousands of individual floes. In the morning we awoke to find our cove piled high with a jumble of icebergs driven our way by the prevailing west wind. The moving ice had broken the lines on three of the six boats which had been tied to the pier, shoving them up on the shore; the boats whose lines hadn't parted had been lifted and tipped as the ice moved beneath them. There was ice on the pier and in the boats, but no real damage.

For half a mile the lake was a solid mass of ice floes, but beyond the first island we could see the dark shimmering of open water. In the afternoon the prevailing wind shifted to the east, gradually releasing the pressure on the ice.

Within an hour open water appeared in the cove, and soon there was room to maneuver a boat. Because our dogfood, flamo, and milk supplies were low, I decided to make a trip to the Chalet. It took me half an hour to push and chop my way through the jumbled floes, but I finally made my way down the ice-choked channel and into the nearly filled lower lake. By the time I returned, just before dusk, the channel was again impassable with ice, and I was forced to leave the boat safely docked beyond its reach in Lower Granite and walk home. The wind, as expected, had shifted back to the west and our harbor was once more packed solidly with ice. I hoped our pier would survive the strain.

Piers in the basin are vulnerable the year around to destructive forces. In the winter there is the crushing weight of drifted snow and the grip of the ice. In spring there is the battering of the breakup. In summer they must absorb the pounding of storm-driven breakers, and in autumn, when they stand naked and exposed, there is the force of buffeting winds. But the greatest menace to our wooden piers is flood.

The worst floods come in winter or very early spring. When solid ice grips a pier and a tropical storm dumps rain instead of snow, something has to give. Once snowmelt and rain build up on the ice they inevitably find a way to get underneath, lifting the frozen sheet—along with everything clutched in its grasp. No one I know has ever been in the basin during one of these floods but they are not uncommon. There were two in our first five years at the cabin.

In March of our third year, on patrol with Jorgy I was astounded to see that the basin's snow slopes, usually velvet smooth, were corrugated vertically into millions of icy gullies. A six-foot-wide strip of ice that rimmed both lakeshores was fractured in a way that suggested it might have been lifted and then dropped. The covering of snow on the ice had been soaked and then refrozen, giving it a granular appearance.

The twenty-five-foot outer span of our pier had been lifted from its foundations and thrown into the cove, where it lay splintered and embedded in the frozen snow. The span's outer crib, a stout-timbered framework filled with tons of rock and concrete, had been shoved inshore a foot and tipped. The identical crib that had supported the span's middle was so completely demolished that none of it remained above the ice.

The following fall, as soon as the water was down, Jorgy and his crew rebuilt the pier, only to have the same thing happen two winters later, this time in January. Tropical storms dumped warm rain on the mountains for several weeks, and heavy cold storms immediately followed. When Jorgy and I reached the cabin several months later, in late April, we found the pier's outer span destroyed again.

But the real shock came when we inspected the cabin. Windrows of flotsam, including huge logs, were piled against its base. Sections of pier, firewood, and branches, all lifted by the flood, had been carried more than eighty feet inland and deposited five feet above normal high water. The midwinter flood had risen to within six inches of the cabin's floor! It was difficult to imagine the cabin sitting in a lake full of milling logs and ice floes, but there was no other explanation. High water markings on the floor joists still remain; so does the layer of pine needles left behind on the foundations when the flood waters receded.

Evidently, the deluge of warm rain melted so much snow that a lake formed on top of the ice, loosening its connection to the shore. The lighter submerged ice, free then to move, rose to the surface so violently it shattered. The prematurely broken ice was then carried down the lake on the flood, with the help of prevailing winds, to form a dam in the mouth of the channel. As the warm rains continued, pouring tons of snowmelt into the basin, the lake apparently rose five feet behind the dam of broken ice. How long the flood lasted and how quickly it subsided will never be known because no one was in the basin to see.

When we cleaned up the remains of the pier, we wondered if

it wasn't too vulnerable to rebuild, but Jorgy's crew appeared in the fall to reconstruct it. We agreed, however, we wouldn't rebuild again. Ten years have passed and the old pier still stands —battered, sagging, splintered but intact. Hardly a year passes without damage and repair, and every fall I inspect it when the water goes down and add the extra bracing its weak spots require. And whenever I reach the cabin in winter or spring I'm a little surprised to find it still standing.

Though the second winter flood destroyed many piers and damaged several cabins, it had one positive aspect. It brought us a table. As soon as the lower lake ice went out that spring we were ready to move into the cabin, so ours was the first boat up the channel that year. Grounded in shallow water just below Upper Granite, stood a stout picnic table with benches attached. It was one of a half dozen that had stood on Picnic Island, half a mile up the lake, and it apparently had floated off the island in the flood. It was beautifully made (at government expense) of three-inch planks stoutly bolted together and must have weighed two hundred pounds. It was just what we needed for the deck beside the pier, so we decided to exercise maritime salvage rights.

Once our gear was unloaded I backed the boat down the channel alongside the table, attached a tow rope and started pulling. The table moved off the gravel bar and started to follow. I thought the job was going to be easy. But then it veered toward the rocks and I had to cut the power. When I started again the prop caught the tow rope, winding it in and killing the motor. By the time the prop was free and the rope refastened, Freda had come to help. I stationed her in the boat and directed her towing while I waded waist-deep to guide the table through the rocks and out into the lake. After an hour of towing we reached the pier—feeling as though we had landed a whale.

With ropes we lifted one end of the table onto the pier. How we got the other end of that waterlogged monster out of the lake is something neither of us can explain. It still seems impossible. But there it sits exactly where we placed it that day. Though it is now bone-dry after ten years of weathering, I still find it hard to lift one end.

Another spring, somewhat by accident, I built a sizeable addition to the pier. During the previous summer I had designed a device to make it easy to get in and out of our two kayaks without falling in the lake: a floating ramp in a narrow slip to be incorporated in an addition to the pier. Before the end of summer I had drawn my plans, hauled all the lumber, and stacked it on the pier. I had planned to build as soon as the water went down in the fall, but that year the spillway wasn't opened until October. When heavy snowstorms followed, it was too late to start and I resigned myself to postponing the project a full year.

But the winter was light and when I skied to the cabin on a lovely day in April, it occurred to me I might be able to build before the ice went out and the lake refilled for summer. The construction site, usually buried under six-foot drifts, was surprisingly open, and there was only two feet of snow on the ice. First I shoveled out the lumber pile so the sun could melt its coating of ice, then I went to work on the pier site itself. As I cleared away the loose snow I piled it up to form a wall that I hoped would function as a windbreak. Before I left I made arrangements with Mike for a few hours of help the following weekend—if the weather stayed fair.

When I arrived a week later it was blowing and cold and a white sky suggested that snow was on the way. Mike was nowhere to be found so I opened and warmed the cabin, ate my lunch, and took a nap. When I awoke the wind had died and the sky looked brighter. I put on two pairs of gloves and all my extra clothes, gathered my tools, and went outside to see what I could do. I was pleased to see the lumber had dried and the job site was completely free of snow—for the moment.

Building a pier is a two-man job because it takes two pairs of hands to hold supporting posts plumb and nail them into a structure. Mike was still missing but at least I could chop postholes in the ten-inch-thick ice. Then I made a discovery: when I tried a post in a tight-fitting hole I found the ice would hold it erect. One after another I forced my posts through the ice, using a leveled string as my guide. If a post was too long I marked it, carefully withdrew it, cut it shorter and replaced it. If a post proved too short I dropped small stones through the hole until it fit. By the time the sun went down, driving me inside, all my deepwater posts were nailed in place and reasonably plumb. I went to bed that night quite pleased with myself.

The next day was bright and clear and the sun on the ice was dazzling. Mike arrived to help, just as I was trying to figure out how to set posts where there wasn't any ice. Within an hour the basic framework was complete. I spent half the afternoon building the slip in the center of my structure, adding extra bracing and piling rock around the feet of the inshore posts. After worrying about the stability of my icebound posts, I realized that now I could chop the holes larger, and drop in enough rock to provide some protection against the spring breakup.

When the job was done I had the skeleton of a ten-foot pier, with a two-foot-wide slip in the middle. At somewhere near high-water level was a tilting ramp, hinged at the back and hung by two ropes in front. It was a strange-looking affair, and I had no idea if it would work. I didn't even know if it would still be there after the ice went out. Enthusiastic cross bracing left me short of planking for the deck, so I used what I had on the outboard edge. Then I carried out several hundred pounds of rock in hopes of anchoring my creation against the pressure of ice floes and the possible flotation of flood.

For once my fears proved needless. The kayak slip and dock not only survived the spring breakup, it worked exactly as envisioned. Before summer was far advanced kayakers from both lakes began to drop by for the pleasure of running their boats high and dry on the ramp, stepping out to stretch their legs, and then propelling themselves out the slip into the lake. And the use of our own kayaks must have doubled.

One of our chief delights in the spring is kayaking through the ice just before it breaks up. Every year, if the weather is mild, there are three or four days when the ice is intact but severely cracked, leaving miles of more or less navigable channels. If we're lucky enough to be at Granite at the time, my daughter Kath and I spend most of the day on the ice. Wearing bathing suits and lifejackets, we thread our way through narrow branching leads in the maze in our flat-bottomed kayaks, "Blue" and "Green."

The ten-foot fiberglass hulls make fine battering rams, while the metal-edged, paddles are good for chopping rotten ice. And if we take a thirty-foot run at a floe we can slide from the water up onto the ice. The only danger comes when ice on just one side of the boat collapses, causing the kayak to roll.

Before the leads are sufficiently open to allow wide-ranging exploration we amuse ourselves, if the weather is warm, with carving "icebergs" off the pack's melting front and guiding them down the channel to their destruction. More exciting still is riding the channel to the middle pool, weaving among the fast-moving floes, then escaping the current before it can pull us into the cataract below. Paddling back upstream through the torrent at the narrows takes all the strength and concentration I can muster, and more than once as I inched my way upstream, paddling furiously, an ice floe has come around the corner to drive me back.

One Memorial Day weekend the lake was perfect for exploring and Kath and I were in our kayaks while three of her friends were trying to follow in a leaky old scow. Their father, Walter, after watching for awhile, launched a canoe and paddled out to join us. He was trying to force his way up a still frozen lead when the ice beneath one side of the canoe collapsed. The canoe quickly rolled and Walter was thrown into the lake. He scrambled up onto a floe but it sank beneath his weight as I paddled madly toward him, trying to direct him to a nearby underwater rock.

By the time he found it and climbed safely on top, his wife Marian was already rowing out in the scow, supplied with towels and blankets. No more than ten minutes after falling in the lake, Walter, draped in blankets, was vigorously rowing back to shore to get warm. By the time I had righted his sunken canoe and towed it back to the pier, he was dressed in dry clothes and drinking hot cocoa, ready to return to the game.

Spring has a tantalizing way of advancing, stopping, retreating into winter, then advancing again as the days grow gradually longer. One mild, quiet day in the middle of May, Freda and I walked up the trail to the cabin under almost summerlike conditions. Slopes exposed to the sun were nearly free of snow, and every bay and cove in both lakes held open water. The ice was riddled with cracks and every day we saw the pack recede a little farther from shore. In fact, a canoe following the shore could probably have navigated the length of the lower lake. A few more days of sun, or one of strong wind, and the pack would break up and quickly melt.

We were sure summer was about to begin, and on our way home we asked Jorgy to get our boat ready so we could move to the cabin the following weekend. It didn't seem possible the ice could last a week. But the following day, we were later to learn, a freak storm slipped down from the gulf of Alaska and settled itself in a low pressure area centered near the basin.

While we enjoyed warm spring weather down below in the city, it was storming and growing colder at Granite. The first few days it rained, eroding the ice, but there wasn't a wind to break up the pack. As the air, cut off from the sun, grew colder the daily rainstorms turned to snow. Nights dropped below freezing, and ice began to form in the cracks between the floes and across the open water in the bays and coves. As the ground quickly cooled new snow began to stick, and old, rainsoaked snow turned to ice.

On Friday night as we were packing for the trip Jorgy called and advised us not to come. He said the ice was getting thicker on what had once been open water, and with snow on the ground the place looked like winter. Even if the weather turned clear overnight (which it did) it would take a good two weeks before the ice went out. His estimate was accurate, almost to the day. A week of winter weather on the threshold of summer had stopped the clock for nearly three weeks.

Many will argue that summer has arrived when both lakes are open. But spring is only gone for good, by my calendar at least, when the last serious snowstorm has passed, usually sometime in June. My reasoning is simple: as long as the basin is cold enough for snow to fall and stick it can't be summer. And there are other unmistakable signs that spring is gone. When more than half the basin is free of melting snow, when the stream beneath the cabin trickles and dies, and when the mating call of the treefrogs no longer fills the night—then summer has clearly arrived.

TWELVE

Autumn

Autumn is a time of beauty and peace, but it means the end of our long blissful summer in the mountains. The days grow shorter and the nights are colder. Once Labor Day has passed most of the summer people are gone and their cabins are shuttered for the winter.

The departure of my friends is always sad, but there are compensations, too. Once summer is over and the lake begins to drop, most motorboats are gone and it is quiet again in the basin. Although the water before long grows too cold for swimming, when the lake goes down a beautiful beach of white sand emerges in Cornell Cove. I like to paddle my canoe over several times each day to spend a few hours building castles with the kids and soaking up the sun.

As the year winds down there is an indescribable spent stillness in the basin that is somehow exquisitely sad. The flowers have wilted, the grass is dead and brown, and all but the largest streams have gone dry. The bright new growth of the hemlocks has faded and turned dusty; shrubbery yellows and wilts, seed pods lie empty, and the squirrels have given up their summer games and turned to the serious business of gathering winter stores. They have felt the gradual cooling as the sun slides farther and farther to the south and they know the time of snow is approaching.

After the first frost, hitherto unnoticed deciduous trees sprinkled through the dark evergreen forests turn warm shades of orange and brown, red and yellow. Easterners accustomed to gaudy displays of maple, oak and beech might scoff at this modest scattering of aspen, ash, willow, and alpine laurel, but it makes a striking change in the basin's mood.

* * *

Before the cabin was rebuilt, when our daughter and dog were still very young, Granite in the fall was something of an adventure. Few cabinowners came in those days. On Monday of the Labor Day weekend the sound of hammers echoed across the basin as shutters were put up and on Tuesday the basin was empty. On freezing mornings we sometimes discovered an inhabited cabin from its column of smoke, and in the evenings soft lamplight from across the lake would reveal another unsuspected neighbor. But often enough the lake was dark, and quite possibly there wasn't another human for thirty, forty, or even fifty miles to the northwest.

In those days it was always a rude surprise to be awakened one mid-September morning by the sound of gunfire echoing across the basin. Deer hunters, for the most part, were packed into the backcountry to elaborate camps, riding horses from Jorgy's corral, but occasionally he took them up the basin by boat. When the lakes were down and the channel impassable, that meant walking them across to our pier. After one victorious marksman dragged the profusely bleeding carcass of his deer the length of our pier, leaving a trail of blood, we complained, and Jorgy obligingly rerouted the traffic. Now that the backpacking boom has spilled over into fall and hunters have become scarce, the basin is quieter and safer than it was a dozen years ago.

In the early years, when the lakes began to drop we moored our motorboat in a protected slip at the Chalet on comparatively loose lines. But if Jorgy failed to retie it every few days the lines would grow too tight and break or the boat would be lashed against the pier where it would rub. If there were rainstorms the danger was increased. Once the boat broke free and drifted onto the rocks. Several times tight lines caused the dock pilings to grind holes through the hull. And twice the boat sank to the bottom in storms.

After several years and considerable fall damage we followed the example of most other lakers and gave our boat to Jorgy for winter storage when we went home after the Labor Day weekend, relying on a Chalet taxi to get us up and down the lake on fall trips. When Jorgy's fall hunting trips made taxi service undependable, we bought a little fiberglass boat to regain our independence. We shared it with Skip, who supplied an old outboard and provided winter storage in his lower lake boathouse.

The first time I tried to use it to take the family up the lake it nearly sank. The wind was blowing hard when we reached the lake and a surf was breaking in the harbor. The boat, half beached, was full of water and covered by an inch of ice. When it was emptied and ready Freda and Kath got in somewhat reluctantly and I piled our parcels around them. I took off my shoes and waded out until the boat was floating, then jumped in and started the engine.

But when we chugged from the harbor and into the big waves beyond, the boat was sluggish and we took water over the bow from every breaker, no matter how I shifted the load. After a hundred yards the hull was ankle deep, the ladies were complaining, the groceries were floating, and it was clear that we weren't going to make it up the lake. I angled for shore and jumped out on a boulder to steady the bobbing boat while Freda and Kath gratefully disembarked. It's a wonder no one fell in the lake. As they scrambled toward the trail to walk to the cabin, I set forth again in the lightened boat. But it still seemed sluggish, and it was all I could do to get it up the lake through the whitecaps to the channel.

By then I suspected what was wrong. I removed the plugs from the three large air tanks and looked inside. All were filled to the brim with water! Instead of buoyancy, they'd provided unwanted ballast. I took off the motor, dragged the boat ashore and turned it upside down to drain. The next day, when I launched it, it floated like a feather, but when it came time to leave Freda and Katherine preferred to walk.

*　*　*

Granite Lake cabins, no matter how well they're built, take a terrific beating from the elements, and fall is the time to make repairs. The dryness of the climate, extremes of temperature, and the weight and wetness of the snow leave scars every year. Nails pull out, boards warp and shrink, and wind-driven snow and hail deeply etch exposed siding, shakes, and shingles. Snow blackens buried wood, soaking timbers rot, and the weight of settling drifts in the spring breaks even the biggest beams.

Doors, decks, and outdoor steps need frequent repair and replacement. Most nails need redriving every two or three years, and the cabin's windward side needs frequent coats of oil to keep the wood from drying out and eroding in the wind. At first, using a big painter's brush on the rough, thirsty shakes, I found oiling an endless, backbreaking task. And filling all the cracks meant wasting gallons of oil. But the last time we oiled the cabin it took my friend Bill and me just four hours and ten gallons of boiled linseed oil. Bill used a long-handled fluffy paint roller, dipped in a tin tub, to roll the half of the cabin that was planked in smooth siding, finishing the cracks and window frames with a brush. Meanwhile, I used a backpack pump with an adjustable nozzle to spray an even coat of oil on the shingles and shakes.

Every fall, once the lake is down, I inspect the sagging and battered old pier to see how much bolstering and propping will be needed to get it through another winter—and, hopefully, the summer beyond. One year I used a turnbuckle and cable to tie the deck to the cribbing. Another fall I rigged a hoist to lift the drooping outer span enough to install new support posts. Most recently I jacked up the inner span to realign posts knocked askew by wind-driven ice. The annual miracle of the pier's survival depends on repairs like these.

Fall is also the time to make repairs on our fleet—when the weather is warm. Patching fiberglass boats requires seventy-degree heat, while sixty degrees is warm enough for revarnishing paddles, oars, and canoe or rowboat rails. Most fiberglassing and varnishing take place on the loft porch when the air is still and in the sunny loft itself when the wind is blowing. With six boats to maintain, there is always one that needs attention. When I tire of patching boats, oiling the cabin, and shoring up the pier I go for a walk in the wilderness.

Fall is traditionally the time to get in firewood. On our side of the channel, where trees are precious for their shade and shelter, firewood is scarce. Our first summer we fueled the wood stove with the last of an old woodpile and fire-damaged lumber from a neighbor's cabin. The next few years there was plenty of scrap lumber from our roof-raising and remodeling. The pair of lodgepoles that nearly fell on the cabin stretched the supply another two years, after which I bought a chainsaw and cut up old downed trees, driftwood, and the logs that had served the previous owners as a dock.

But after ten years and the construction of a fireplace, our woodpile was gone, and so apparently were our burnable resources. Then one day I noticed more than a dozen logs in the shallow water of the channel pool. A few were barely floating, but most were lying on the bottom. Twenty years before a log boom had been built to block the swamp from my neighbor's harbor, but now it was in ruins and he said he'd be glad to see it go. I didn't know if salvage was worthwhile, but I waded out into the mud-bottomed swamp to jab the logs with a crowbar and found them surprisingly sound. I also found I could move every log. Even the sinkers lying in the mud seemed to retain some buoyancy.

Several days later, with Mike's help, I was ready to start. We cleared a tunnel through the swamp to a clearing, chained a "come along" to a large pine, and assembled a collection of heavy ropes, axe, saw, hammer, and several large prybars. Wading in the swamp we put a rope around each log in turn and dragged it inshore as far as we could. Lying there in the mud, with one end above the surface, they looked like a family of crocodiles.

The log nearest the tunnel we lashed with our heaviest rope to the winch. Mike cranked while I lifted with a prybar. The rope grew taut, then snapped. We tried again with the smallest log, doubled the rope, and successfully inched the black, slimy torpedo ashore. When a second small log was landed we swung both around to build an elevated drying rack in the clearing. After that the job went smoothly. During the week that followed, aided by curious neighbors and friends, I managed to winch ashore all thirteen logs and roll them down the drying rack.

It was a full month before the logs were dry on the surface, and I waited until nearly September to buck them into twenty-inch rounds. Even then they were soaked inside, although the wood seemed sound and hard. It was late September before I split the rounds into fireplace-size chunks. Water spurted up at each stroke of the axe. The sodden chunks were spread in the clearing so each got full sun. Two weeks later when I visited again, I turned each piece over. I waited until the last fall trip of the year, in late October, before carrying my still damp and heavy firewood from the clearing and stacking it near the cabin. The following spring the wood was finally dry and burned beautifully—better than firewood that hadn't spent twenty years underwater!

Encouraged by this success, several years later I seized another salvage logging opportunity. Late in August a rainstorm deluged the basin, raising the level of the upper lake three or four inches above normal high water. When the rain stopped and the sun came out, I bailed the canoe and paddled to Cornell Cove. To my surprise, two old logs that had been grounded for years in the shallows had floated free. Before other scavengers could pounce, I paddled home, tossed several coils of rope in the motorboat and returned. By sunset the logs were moored to trees in our cove.

The next morning, Kath and I set forth in kayaks to prospect the shallow coves beneath the avalanche chutes for more floaters. We found five small logs and towed them all to the harbor. This time we didn't need to winch them ashore. We lashed them tightly in the shallows and left for the summer. By the time I returned three weeks later it was fall and the lake had dropped three feet leaving the logs high and dry. Removing the straining ropes, I bucked them into rounds, which I rolled up onto the lawn above high water, to be split the following summer. These two salvage operations yielded a woodpile that, stretched by coal, should last five or six years.

Every few years, usually in October, we are deluged by countless miles of spiderweb. Strands hundreds of feet long ride the breeze down the lake to festoon the trees around the cabin. Backlighted against the shadowed cliffs to the west, its mass seems enormous, as though just beyond the ridge the country must be crawling with madly spinning spiders. Perhaps, as with the mice, there are periodic spider population explosions. Standing on the pier I am constantly clearing the strands from my face. On a dewy morning the web-wrapped trees are strung with tiny dewdrop lights. For a few days, no more, spider web is everywhere, then the wind that brought it carries it away. Never in all the miles of drifting, floating strands have I seen a single spider.

The biggest undertaking of the year is closing up for winter. In the gentle summer we live mostly outdoors, so there's a lot to move into the shelter of the cabin before the deep crushing snows arrive.

Closing up the first year was a simple procedure, partly because we wouldn't be back before late spring and partly because we didn't know what to do. We didn't know, for instance, that mice and other creatures would hold a party all winter—knocking bottles off shelves, gnawing through boxes and excavating mattresses—unless poison grain was liberally spread to hold down their numbers. We didn't know that carbonated drinks and certain canned foods expand when they freeze and explode their containers. We didn't know that the smallest crack would admit enough wind-driven snow to form a drift.

So that year I climbed a ladder to cover the two stovepipes with buckets and tighten the guy wires that held them. We swung the hinged shutters closed and hooked them from inside, bundled up the things we wanted to take home and swept the floor. Once the cabin was locked, with everything inside, there was nothing more to do.

When we began to acquire more boats, when the cabin was plumbed for water and gas, and when we began to visit in the winter, the procedure became more complex. The first two years after the loft was built I braced its flat roof with posts in case Jorgy was wrong about the west wind preventing the buildup of snow. I also nailed plywood over all the windows—until I found I needed light more than protection. As the cabin was developed it became easier to forget things. An autumn never passed without my forgetting to turn off the gas, or lock the outhouse, or close the bathroom window, or take home the box of food I had carefully cleaned from the refrigerator. One year I left out the canoe; another time it was the pump. And more than once, when the weather was fine and I expected to return the following weekend, I foolishly left the water on and suffered broken pipes in the subsequent deep freeze.

Finally I was driven to make a checklist of essential tasks. Over the years the list has been refined, added to, and subdivided. Nowadays the task of closing, if undertaken all at once, would be a backbreaking job. But since there isn't any hurry I spread it out over several months, doing a little at a time, so it doesn't seem like work. "Progressive closing," I call it, and the process still gives me pleasure.

For simplicity's sake, closing is divided into three stages. Stage one on the checklist is labeled "End of summer." It shows everything that must be done before we leave for the city, assuming the lake will drop before we can return. The biggest job is drydocking our fleet of six boats. The two kayaks are easy: I simply carry them from the pier and leave them upside down on the front deck for fall use. The canoe, which I use more than ever once the lake begins to drop, goes upside down on the pier, wedged against the little tree and the picnic table and lashed to both to keep it safe from the wind.

In the early years we stored our motorboat with Jorgy for autumn, winter and spring, but then we devised a better arrangement, one that gave us more use of the boat when we needed it most. Before the lake drops to close the channel, I strip the boat of its windshield, engine, gas tank and seats, then we drag it across the lawn to a pair of nearby trees where we stand it on its transom on a cushioning tire, and lash it securely in place for the winter.

The greatest struggle at the end of every summer used to be wrestling the sailboat (a thirteen-foot Sunfish) and Kath's rowboat (an elegant twelve-foot skiff) into the loft for the winter. It always meant scraped knuckles, scratched paint, and splintered door jambs. Then, a few years ago, I built a porch-boathouse on the front of the cabin that just barely accommodates the sailboat and rowboat side by side. Mike and I can now stow all three big boats for the winter in half an hour. When all the oars, paddles, lifejackets, oarlocks, gas cans, tools, mast, sail, rudder, centerboard, seats, and bailers are brought in and put away in the loft, the fleet is secure for autumn.

The old double mattress that spends the summer on the pier must be carried to the loft and covered with the heavy plastic sheet used to protect it during summer rainstorms. At the same time we bring in the canvas hammock, the wind chime that hangs in the tree above it, and the set of horseshoes from the pit by the woodpile. Because the next time I arrive it may be cold and raining, I replenish the woodpile by the fireplace. And just before leaving for the summer we judiciously spread several packets of poisoned grain behind the stove and underneath the fridge to start thinning a mouse population that has fattened on the abundant food supply all summer.

Stocking the cabin for winter and spring, with heavy items at least, must be completed before we leave for the summer. Once the channel drops there won't be a flamo run until sometime next June, so I make sure I have three full tanks on hand. I need eight gallons of kerosene for the two heaters, a lamp, and starting winter fires. The Coleman lanterns require two gallons of white gas, and I keep three extra gallons of outboard motor mix for the fall boat. There must be enough left over to get the motorboat down the lake to the Chalet next summer.

Stage two of my closing check list is headed "Mid-fall," when the danger of freezing pipes increases with every week. Sometime in early October, depending on the year, the community pipeline from the spring is shut down before the risk of freezing pipes grows too great. Before this happens I use the pipeline's high pressure to flush out the water heater, and fill the eighty-gallon roof tank with fresh water. Together with the water heater, this gives me one or two weekends of running water after the pipeline from the spring has been drained. It's a gamble, of course, and several times a frozen pipe has burst. But many more times, even after hard freezes, I have enjoyed the luxury of hot showers when all other water systems in the basin were shut down. My record late shower, after a long and mild autumn, was on November tenth, but normally my tanks and pipes are drained by the final week in October.

By midfall the lake is all the way down, and it's wise to make pier repairs as early as possible, to avoid the need to break ice or work in snowstorms. I crawl all over the pier and canoe beneath it to find weak points and shore up bracing. The launching ramp, which would surely be destroyed by drifting snow, is dismantled and laid flat on the pier beside the slip. The sheets of waterproof plywood of the tent platform floor are pried off the stringers and carried to the rear deck and laid flat before a heavy autumn snowstorm can crush the platform.

Making the final close in a snowstorm with several feet of fresh snow on the ground can be a chore, so I try to complete most of the outside work in midfall. I bring in the table that spends the summer on the rear deck, stow its oilcloth-covered stools in the outhouse, fill the emergency woodbin beneath the bunk in the bay, and replenish the woodpile by the fireplace. The outhouse shutters are nailed in place, my three shovels are brought in, the Aladdin wicks are trimmed, the folding chairs are stacked in the parlor, the boat battery is taken down to the city for charging, and winter food is brought in while our fall boat is still in the water.

Winter staples include canned bacon that requires no refrigeration, several six packs of canned beer, small cans of fruit, and enough dried milk to make several gallons. Both the kayaks are stowed in the loft, leaving only the canoe still out on the pier. And just before leaving I hang the shutters on the bay so I won't have to dig them from a snowdrift when I return. One year they were buried so deep I didn't find them until spring!

The last heading on my list is "Final closing." There comes a time when summer can no longer be stretched, when the days are short and the nights are long and cold. To complete the job of closing our cabins, Skip and I make a final fall trip to the basin on November tenth. When we arrive the Chalet is shuttered for the winter, just as it was that day in late October when Freda and I first saw it, and our little boat looks even smaller in the empty harbor. We wear packs this trip, and boots, because we'll have to walk out around the lake. The basin is still and deeply shadowed, even in midday, as we chug up the black, freezing lake. Skip's harbor is shaded in late fall, and as usual we have to break ice as we pole the boat to the boathouse and lift it inside for the winter. There is snow on the ground in the shade as I climb over the hill to my cabin.

My main remaining chore involves bringing in and stowing the tent platform's plywood floor, but since it will block the back door for the winter, I first drag the big outboard motor to the shower and replenish the woodpile by the fireplace one last time. After considerable maneuvering, the back door is locked with the plywood propped against it. From the outside, I nail the door's heavy shutter in place and put up the shutters on the bay. The next time I come this whole end of the cabin will be buried beneath snowdrifts. In the last of the light I put blocks in the sliding windows of the loft to prevent easy entry, then I cross the peninsula to Skip's cabin for dinner.

The next morning when I wake the sun is shining, but three inces of snow have quietly fallen in the night and the harbor shines with a sheet of new ice. Breathing clouds of steam into the still, dry air and carrying a smoking cup of coffee, I go down to the pier, break the ice in the canoe, and empty out water, ice, and snow. Then I launch it again to dry out in the sun, and return for my breakfast and final chores. Skip arrives an hour later, just as I finish, and is happy to join me for a last paddle around the lake's scalloped shore. The morning is so warm we take off our shirts. The lake is steaming and still, and every-where snow is falling from the trees, but the blue winter sky, clear an hour before, is fast filling with clouds by the time we return to the dock.

We lift the canoe from the water and carry it, dripping, to the loft, to store it upside down on top of the bed. While Skip waits, I pull all the curtains, turn off the gas at the winter valve beneath the floor, and lock the doors and the outhouse. Then I pick up my pack and we set off for the trail that circles the lower lake. The track is bare of snow, except in deep shade, but the sun is lost in lowering clouds, and before long a gentle rain begins to fall. The mist descends around us and gusts of wind shove hard at our backs, but it doesn't matter now. We're dressed for stormy weather, the cabins are closed and the car is waiting a mile or two away.

Even if the rain turns to thick, heavy snow we'll have enough time to reach the highway before the Granite road closes. I'm ready now for winter. The boats are put away out of reach of the snow and the cabin is secure and well-stocked. Once Christmas is past a blanket of snow will make traveling easy, and I'll be ready to ski across the frozen lower lake to begin another year at the cabin.